BACKBENCHER'S DILEMMA

BACKBENCHER'S DILEMMA

Paul Rose

FREDERICK MULLER LIMITED
LONDON

First published in Great Britain 1981 by
Frederick Muller Limited, London, NW2 6LE

British Library Cataloguing in Publication Data

Rose, Paul
    Backbencher's dilemma.
    1. Great Britain. Parliament. House of Commons
    2. Great Britain – Politics and government
    – 1964 –
    I. Title
    941.085'6'0924   JN673

    ISBN 0-584-10379-4

Phototypeset by Input Typesetting Ltd., London
Printed in Great Britain by Billing and Sons Ltd., Surrey

Contents

Introduction

In *Backbencher's Dilemma* I do not set out to give a comprehensive account of the work of Parliament, nor do I attempt
to make a thorough-going analysis of all the shortcomings of
Government or of the Labour Party. It is not an autobio-
graphy, although it is a personal and discursive account of
fifteen years in Parliament and what led up to it, highlighting
those aspects which I find most worthy of comment or in
which I took a special interest.

Since Members do not just arrive at Westminster without
motivation or, indeed, without election campaigns, the book
takes a critical look at the M.P.'s job and his relative impo-
tence, and at the secrecy and power of an Executive dominated by the Prime Minister and frequently ruled by civil
servants. It considers the problem of radicals disenchanted
with outmoded attitudes in the Labour Party; it discusses the
electoral system itself and dwells on some of my own
experiences.

I have not sought to base my book on detailed research
into Hansard or learned commentators, although I am grateful to those whom I have quoted. I am equally grateful to
those many newspapers, in particular *The Guardian* and *Contemporary Review*, which published many articles upon which
I have been able to draw. I would also like to thank my
colleagues in Parliament and the media, and the members of
my own Constituency Party who sustained me until my seemingly sudden decision not to seek re-election in 1979. I am
also grateful to the Members of F.A.I.R., the Deo Gloria

Trust and others who assisted me through three harrowing years of harassment in a libel action by a cult.

The result is an inside view of the political process and a consideration of the changes necessary to create more open and responsive Government. It is one more attempt to lift the veil of secrecy and penetrate the outmoded bureaucracy and attitudes which afflict modern political life.

CHAPTER ONE

The Sixty-Nine Rebels

The most traumatic experience for an M.P. virtually born into the Labour Party is to find himself, at one and the same rate isolated from those colleagues with whom he has identified in the past, at odds with his Constituency Party, defying his whips and flouting a Conference decision. The night that happened to me in 1971 was when I followed Roy Jenkins, together with sixty-seven other Labour M.P.s, to vote in favour of accepting the terms of entry negotiated by Mr. Heath's Tory Government, with the E.E.C.

One of Harold Wilson's closest supporters laying his hand on my shoulder, urged me as a good friend not to be naïve. 'There are no principles in politics,' he replied to my apparently pompous assertion that the vote was a matter of principle. 'His Master's voice,' I muttered under my breath, as I considered the pragmatism of the Opposition.

Earlier in the day Reg Freeson, a thoughtful, hard working and intense Member, whom I had known since childhood and for whose stand on race relations and Vietnam I had the utmost respect, had approached me in a more principled way. Like myself, he did not think the Common Market should be an issue to divide the Party ideologically, nor should it attain, as it eventually did, the importance attributed to it as a yardstick of socialist committment. What genuinely concerned him, and others with similarly sincere views was that by dint of voting for entry, Roy Jenkins would be voting in the same lobby as the majority of the Conservative Party while being Deputy Leader of the Labour Party. This would mean that Reg Freeson and other would-be supporters of Jenkins for that position, could no longer bring themselves to vote for him. The enthusiastic support for Jenkins' stand expressed in a demonstration of exuberance at a Party meeting had alike alarmed Party loyalists and those who feared Jenkins' apparent attachment to the right wing of the Party. It prompted an angry response from Wilson himself, only precedented by his 'dog licence' speech directed at those mainly left-wing opponents of his East of Suez policy in the first-ever revolt, in which I myself had participated, against the Labour Government following the 1966 victory.

Whether I had a dog licence or not, my own view was that I was certainly not going to act like a sheep. I had taken part in too many revolts along with the so-called left to be deterred from the deep-seated conviction that now led me towards the lobby with the so-called right. The definitions were no longer meaningful to me after three parliamentary elections and my own observations of political behaviour. What was beginning to matter was the injection into politics of honesty and consistency rather than pragmatism and short-term advantage. I had found that radicalism was not the prerogative of any one pressure group and my active participation on the executive of the Labour Committee For Europe was entirely consistent with my membership of the far-left League for Democracy in Greece. Between 1964 and 1970 I was classified as part of the 'soft' as opposed to the 'hard' left, in this simplistic view of politics.

However, Freeson's cogent argument suggesting a principled abstention had its force. It would maximize the protest and allow others to join it, without bracketing us in the eyes of rank-and-file Party members with the Tories. In the event there were twenty abstentions and numerous reluctant members of that light brigade which fears to antagonize both those on high or the big battalions below.

I approached Roy Jenkins about the suggested abstention, with the caveat that whatever he decided to do I would be with him, but it was worthy of consideration. However, to Roy Jenkins, his Constituency was wider than Stetchford or even the Labour Party. It was a debt of honour to thousands of people who had written to him to support his integrity, and anything less than the semi-suicidal action contemplated that night would be to demean him and his followers. Unhappily honour is not always a viable political asset.

I recall how Stan Orme, an old friend from my formative days in the Manchester political world of the Left Club, Victory for Socialism and the Left Coffee House, informed me from a deep knowledge of Labour Party revolts that, when the chips were down, only thirty Members would have the guts to defy the whips. Ironically Stan, the archetypal rebel, was later to find himself signing internment orders in Northern Ireland before joining the Cabinet in charge of Social Security.

What no one had reckoned with was the way in which the 'Europeans' had given each other mutual support and encouragement, not least by reason of the organizational skill of Bill Rodgers, a formidable opponent and loyal friend. The statements of the former Foreign Secretary Michael Stewart, Harold Lever, George Thomson and George Brown, none of whom were my political heroes, nevertheless had great weight. Each affirmed that the terms negotiated differed little from those we in the Labour Party had been prepared to accept. Shirley Williams also played a major role. I recalled those arduous lecture tours in France, where, because I spoke French fluently, I had been sent by the Foreign Office – to Bordeaux, Agen, Toulouse, Lyons and Le Havre – to plead the cause of British entry in the face of the reluctant De Gaulle. We put forward the offer of British technology and political stability as inducements to the French who feared the effect of a wider community on their own position and the cohesion of the E.E.C. itself. Having French as a common language with my Hungarian-born wife, whom I had met in Paris, was a considerable advantage and I sometimes wonder how much it influenced my 'European' attitudes.

For whatever reason – emotional, internationalist, intellectual, loyalty to Jenkins, or the over-riding idea that it was wrong to oppose in Opposition what one would have done in power – sixty-nine of us reluctantly brushed shoulders with our traditional enemies and found ourselves branded as traitors and right-wing reactionaries. This was said whatever our political antecedents or views on a wide variety of matters which were of more significance than the finely balanced judgment on entry to the Common Market. The pitch of emotion and hostility was reflected in the level to which political debate plunged as I emerged behind Roy Jenkins from the lobby. 'You f . . . ing traitor!' was the cry of one newly-elected member who knew nothing of the period of application when seven Parliamentary Private Secretaries had been summarily dismissed for opposing Harold Wilson's initial decision to apply for membership. Much to my chagrin, I replied in similar terms as to where he should go. An earlier gentle suggestion from a Trade Union leader that I should not commit treason was now being put in harsher terms.

I had debated the issue in depth with this member of the T.U.C. General Council. His opposition was based on premises common to the far left, which equated the E.E.C. as the economic counterpart to NATO. Others used the little Englander argument to the extent that Joan Lester, a sincere opponent of entry on the basis of our prime obligation to the Third World, had openly criticized the willingness of the antis to share applause and slogans with members of the National Front in demonstrations. Curiously, we agreed on every premise but differed on our conclusions and that was the ultimate and only point of divergence, since Europe for Europe's sake was as abhorrent a concept to me as the little Englander mentality echoed so articulately by Peter Shore.

I also felt disillusioned with an old hero, Tony Wedgwood Benn, whose acute observation is too often dismissed by the mass media as the mouthings of an ogre or a fanatic. I was standing at the centre of the tea room when the news reached me that the Tories were having a free vote. Tony came up alongside. I had been privileged to be one of the first to read his plan for a referendum on entry to the E.E.C. which he had devised when still a 'European' in order to avoid a split in the Party. I had found it unacceptable and reluctantly returned it with that message. When I told him the news of the Tory free vote his face turned ashen and he inexplicably remarked, 'Call that democracy!' Tony Benn is a charming and much maligned man, but I still find his judgment on Europe incomprehensible.

What occured to me was that he feared a free vote in the Labour Party when, along with Peter Shore, he was riding on the popular tide of anti-Common Market feeling, above the heads of the Parliamentary Party, much as Enoch Powell was doing on Immigration. Both, in their own way, were populists with a power base outside the House of Commons. Benn's reaction now seemed as irrational as it was unexpected but the Labour free vote never materialized as it was voted down by a P.L.P. meeting in which the most effective voice denouncing it was that of Reg Prentice, later to renounce the Party itself in the name of freedom and switch sides on Europe as well. Such are the ironies of politics.

It was a tragedy for the Party that this rift destroyed rational thought and was turned into a re-run of the left-right division which had wrecked the Party under Gaitskell and which only Gaitskell's opposition to entry had begun to heal. His associate, Douglas Jay, became the guardian of the Ark of that covenant, notwithstanding Baroness Gaitskell's assertion that her husband would no longer have held that view.

Thus a curious alliance of the far left was forged with the conservative right of the Labour Party. It was reflected in my own constituency and was precisely the alliance that James Callaghan had made a play for, prior to 1970, when *In Place of Strife* was opposed by the Trade Union Movement at large and the left of the Party in particular. That he made his views known while still a member of a Cabinet pledged to its support, was a measure of Callaghan's political agility which acute observers did not under-rate.

It was however more curious that, only a short time before that traumatic night, twenty-five Labour M.P.s who were broadly of the left and centre left had advertized their support for entry in *Tribune*. They included such names as Eric Heffer, who more than anyone had influenced my own ideas on the basis of an old-fashioned internationalism, mirrored in the slogan of the Italian Socialist Party: '*Per un Europa Unità e Socialista*'. There was Stan Newens, a sincere if sometimes naïve fighter for every leftist cause; and Sid Bidwell whose

7

stand on race relations had made him a bitter enemy of the National Front. They all had in common a background of membership of dissident Marxist organizations influenced by Trotsky. On the other hand, there were radical individualists like Andrew Faulds and Leo Abse; while the Tribune Group member Les Huckfield had attended the pro-E.E.C. faction meetings until the eleventh hour before the vote. His late conversion left me breathless but the rationale for many was the conviction that it was more important to keep faith with their own natural supporters than to stand out on the E.E.C. issue. To me this was the greatest tragedy in polarizing the Party along traditional lines.

Michael Barnes, a bright young addition to the front bench, and I had shared the same radical views on such issues of foreign policy as Rhodesia, Vietnam, the Middle East and Biafra. We also agreed on Europe and announced our feelings at a Party meeting chaired by Douglas Houghton where, together with the late Professor John Mackintosh, we explained the events, not least the powerlessness in isolation of the 1964 Labour Government, which had led us to that position. Douglas Houghton, also a European with some influence, commented that it sounded more like a revivalist meeting than a debate but the road to Europe was as strewn with the development of such ideas and with conversions on the road to and from Brussels. The significance of that division is the stultifying effect it has had upon the development of new radical ideas in the Party.

For the dissidents on the front bench seven examples were to suffice to match the seven Parliamentary Private Secretaries who were sacked for doing precisely the opposite when Labour was in power. Cledwyn Hughes, Will Edwards, Michael Barnes, David Marquand, Bill Rodgers, Dickson Mabon and I had all received identical marching orders. Of these seven, two survived to become ministers again and while Will Edwards and Michael Barnes lost their seats. Cledwyn Hughes, David Marquand and I have voluntarily relinquished ours. Others, like David Owen, later to become Foreign Secretary, and Bob Maclennon resigned their frontbench positions to be reinstated in Government, the latter as junior minister to Shirley Williams. The unhappy result for me was that my first love, and major ambition, a junior post at the Home Office, was denied to me. The writing was on the wall and I realized almost subliminally that I should prepare for a future outside the parliamentary arena. It precipitated me back to practising my profession as a barrister as an insurance policy, and to a greater emphasis on one of the more emotionally rewarding aspects of parliamentary life, the ability to communicate ideas through writing.

I tried to analyze the malaise of a Party with a new type of intake, which had swept the board in 1966 only to lose out in 1970 – divided by loyalties rooted in the 1930s rather than the realities of the 1970s – and steadily losing its mass support in large parts of the country. This realization is gradually affecting the thinking of commentators and Professor David Marquand has termed the current situation the 'Politics of nostalgia'. The other side of the coin was the reaction in my Constituency Party. A meagre postbag slightly favoured entry but, while four of my six officers supported me, I knew only too well the hostile feelings of two-thirds of my management committee and three out of four of the wards. It was the first clash in a remarkably united Party in which differences were sunk in a common effort to win and make this marginal seat a Labour stronghold.

To my embarrassment, one ward congratulated me on my stand, a clear provocation to my opponents. The Constituency Agent and Secretary, Alison Kelly, whose great organizational ability had made the seat one of the few in the country where the Tories looked like amateurs, supported me. Our dour, hard-headed Treasurer from the same ward was passionately in favour, as was the young Minute secretary, while one of the Vice-Chairmen, an amiable headmaster, also agreed. By contrast the Party Chairman and the other Vice-Chairman, both active Trade Unionists, opposed.

There was a clear difference in age, class and political spectrum. The older, more working-class members of the traditional right and left were against. The newer elements, socially mobile and conscious of the international scene, were in favour. Even the young socialist militants of the far left were strongly ambivalent in the face of their internationalist slogans and the realities of the battle.

In the event, a motion to call for my resignation, supported by two normally mutually antagonistic stalwarts from the wings in the Crumpsall Ward which nominated me in 1962, was withdrawn. Another highly critical motion went the same way and a mild rap over the knuckles reflected sorrow rather than anger in a Party where personal relations had always been good, whatever the stridency of political debate.

I recognized the right of those who selected me to dismiss me – compulsory reselection is unnecessary, however, for M.P.s should not anyway be rubber stamps. My committee had supported other rebellions and could not expect me always to follow their line. Thus they reluctantly accepted, not least because of common battles fought in the past, my reputation for hard constituency work and, to quote the speech which summed up the situation for them, 'Paul may have been a bloody fool but we could have a much worse M.P.' Praise indeed!

More strange was the almost Orwellian situation in the House of Commons where, suddenly, one became an unperson. The power and patronage of leadership was underlined. The grapevine of informers among one's so-called comrades was exposed. The nomination for the Council of Europe delegations abroad or interesting tasks at home, standing and select committees, facility of pairing and other weapons which made life more pleasant, reposed behind the closed doors of the whips' office. The tyranny of the whips had been liberalized by John Silkin and Brian O'Malley, but the grey men began to reassert themselves. After all, who wants to be a whip? It means a self-denying ordinance on self-expression and a role more akin to a policeman and a statistician.

It was this futile internecine strife over a desolate terrain, and with a strategy as outmoded as the Maginot line, that prompted me to look at what I termed 'Labour's mid-term Blues' in *Contempory Review*. The article was an attempt to break through the arid battles of the old right and old left, which failed to acknowledge the vast, if subtle, changes in the composition of the population and nuances of class that had overtaken the battle lines of the 1930s, and which I felt the Party had failed to recognize in its 1970 campaign. Indeed the analysis was even more appropriate to the subsequent demise of the simplistic Callaghan (Trade Union) approach to politics, which precipitated the Labour Party into the abyss in the 1979 election.

My argument for a new approach in line with these changed conditions elicited some surprise from colleagues who had not read my articles before. Strange how the life of an M.P. tends to make one so egocentric as to read only selectively and indulge in narcissistic re-reading of one's own contributions to debate in Hansard and the Press. Like similar pleas from like-minded Members, this viewpoint caused hardly a ripple – the reason being that attitudes are often so deeply entrenched amongst many activists that they do not even begin to understand what some of us are trying to say, with the result that the radical and the young find other outlets for their idealism. Callaghan or Williams v. Benn is one battle with which they cannot readily identify and about which they have little enthusiasm and last Summer's references to 'the gang of three' hardly elevated the tone of debate.

I called for a more modern approach in the same way that Michael Barnes was to do in *Labour Weekly* while David Marquand outlined the current 'politics of nostalgia' in his inaugural lecture at Salford University. All round the fringes of the Party were plenty of people who were waiting for this, but not at its heart where it really matters and will continue to matter until the Party is forced to modernize or die.

Loss of power is a shock to the complex and fragile nervous system of a major political party. Prolonged deprivation of power sometimes produces withdrawal symptoms, a cycle of unusual responses, inner tensions and erratic behaviour replacing normal political drive. That is one obvious diagnosis for the corporate and individual malaise which afflicted the Labour Party from Rochdale via Uxbridge to Lincoln and the thinly populated benches at Westminister between 1970 and 1974 and, once again, in the internicine strife of 1979–80.

However, that is only one of the contributory causes of

Labour's uncertainty in presenting itself as the natural alternative Government. Certainly there is widespread disillusionment in the electorate with Government policies, particularly in the economic field, and this frequently extends to a mistrust of all promises and all parties.

Whatever the results of G.L.C. and Municipal elections – and Labour has largely proved to be odds-on favourite – a significant finding of the Polls, borne out to a degree by the bye-elections, was that more people would vote Liberal given the chance of a Liberal win than actually intend to vote Labour. This was not a phenomenon related directly to Labour's performance in office. To make that analysis would be to deny spectacular victors in bye-Elections at Bromsgrove, or the swing at Hayes and Harlington, the closest neighbour to Uxbridge. It is therefore a more recent development.

The advocates of a centre party may suggest that everyone is running for the solid middle ground. The truth is more complicated. There is undoubtedly a public revulsion from machine politics and extreme slogans. More significant, however, is the credibility gap that divides a significant progressive section of the electorate from commitment to the major Opposition party. Its antics in Opposition have earned it the scepticism and occasionally the contempt of this articulate and growing sector of opinion. When sixty-nine of us chose over Europe to defy local party machines, the National Conference and the Party whip, it was a principle over and above the individual issue which was at stake.

We argued then that there was a need to reaffirm integrity and consistency in politics, and that action has preserved the possibility of regaining that support. Some wounds are healing. But when the press turned sour on him, the Party leader, Harold Wilson, was pilloried beyond decent limits for having faced one way, then for having sat on the fence playing the oracle, before finally turning a spectacular somersault while attempting to prove his consistent immobility.

His motive was to preserve the unity of the Party in the face of gigantic pressures. Compromise was elevated into a principle. In the sense that the surface skin only was scratched at Lincoln, he succeeded, and he repulsed an all-out commitment to leave the E.E.C. which threatened to tear the Labour Party apart. The result was an untenable formula which no one took seriously. Nevertheless, internal haemorrhage can be more serious if less obvious, and many Labour backbenchers bleed a little every time they recall these events. They still hold the view that strong and resolute leadership would have carried the overwhelming majority of the Parliamentary Party, and most of the constituencies. Some major unions would have made life difficult temporarily, but ultimately Mr. Wilson would have emerged with an unassailable coalition behind him. His reputation for trickiness would have been scotched, and a real rather than a spurious unity would have resulted.

Mr. Wilson's actions are easier to understand if one recalls the traumatic Gaitskell Clause 4 episode and the nuclear disarmament controversies. At that time there were two distinctly delineated and ideologically opposed factions. What Mr. Wilson and others have failed to recognize since is the increased sophistication of M.P.s and the electorate, who are less doctrinaire and more fluid in relation to individual issues. There were painful memories of more recent strife with the Trade Unions and sections of the Party only a year before the very election which tipped Labour out of office in 1970.

The legacy of Mrs. Barbara Castle's attempt to convince the Party of the necessity of *In Place of Strife* cast a shadow over Labour's first crucial battle thereafter in Opposition, which still hangs over its ambivalent attitude to industrial relations. The electorate is able to discern this through the verbal formulae that provide an incomplete answer. In bending over backwards to atone for her past, Mrs. Castle's naturally biting and effective style only resulted in her making the most reasonable sound unreasonable. Her objections to the irrelevant, unworkable and divisive Industrial Relations Act, which the Tories introduced that same year, 1970, were couched in terms designed only to appeal to those most offended by her previous actions. Thus a courageous and talented Minister of Transport was miscast in a role that led her to the back benches, bereft of support from those whom she sought most eagerly to placate.

In the effort of resisting the Act, the Parliamentary Labour Party was drained of much of its energy. It devoted almost all of its time to an issue upon which the battleground had been chosen by the enemy and fought day and night in a vigorous but inevitably vain onslaught against the superior numbers in the division lobbies. Indeed, the necessity for opposition to divisive legislation, such as the Housing Finance Act, created negative responses and little time for creative policy making.

Fighting the industrial relations battle, sometimes brilliantly, and at other times with slogans more appropriate to the 1930s, the steering committee took a foolish pride in the physical stamina exhibited in four hundred laps of the lobbies, rather than in spelling out a coherent alternative philosophy for industrial relations and prices and incomes policy. The struggle left three-line whips devalued and Parliament exhausted for a considerable period. In a curious sense the after-effects have not altogether worn off. Labour won the arguments and lost the votes. For a year or more following this, the Party was rather like a long-distance runner who had started the marathon too fast.

One result of that period and of subsequent actions is that the public is suspicious that Labour has become no more than a creature of powerful trade union interests. That would not matter since the trade union connection is vital; but what is becoming increasingly apparent is that the most underprivileged in our society – the old, the sick, the immigrants, the women, the disabled, the unemployed, the large families of the lower paid – are frequently the least protected by union militancy. It is a problem which socialists and trade unionists must examine urgently to produce a socialist approach to incomes policy.

This implies a viable programme for the elimination of poverty and a closing of the gap between rich and poor. It can only come about in an atmosphere of a society seen positively to be moving towards greater social justice and public control of the economy. Labour must demonstrate its ability when in office to persuade the Unions voluntarily to impose self-restraint. There is no statutory or mystical alternative. That is why the Labour Party tends to be more radical in opposition than when in office; and why the term 'left' is so inappropriate to some of the most conservative elements in the Party. The latter do not recognize the complex countervailing pressures, the competing interest groups, the increasingly blurred class lines in our society. The growing number of socially mobile open-minded young people, who would vote Labour in a reasonably good year, is becoming an increasingly important electoral factor which they have not recognized. Outmoded slogans may still rally the old faithful, but they are alien to the rest of the voters. Elections are won and lost in marginal seats precisely where this new and more volatile voter is significant. In 1964 to some degree, and above all in 1966, these people voted Labour. They do not seek to inhibit the radicalism of Labour, nor do they regard socialism as a dirty word so long as it is disentangled from its connotations of bureaucracy and authoritarian attitudes.

It is not therefore an old-fashioned left-right struggle that now afflicts the Labour Party. It is rather an argument about the style of leadership and politics that is demanded by those electors and by those of us who seek to win their respect. They will not respect those who twist and turn with every short-term popular prejudice. A propensity to lead and to look at the longer term is vital. They can make nothing of a Party which pursues a policy of abstentionism in European institutions, where decisions are increasingly being made or influenced. They are unlikely to be impressed by the ambivalence of leadership on the token strike called on 1 May 1980. They demand greater selectivity in our approach to industrial disputes within the context of a philosophy of incomes as well as of prices.

Above all, they will be suspicious of a Party which appears to act in Opposition in a way quite obviously different from that in which it acted and would act in Government. They do not expect responsible representatives to stand on their political heads after years of campaigning on an issue central to the future location and mode of political struggle. They are unlikely to be impressed at the virtual punishment of those refusing such undignified contortions.

Labour, on the showing of Mr. Heath, won in 1973 by default without having first charted a five-year course and now it could win on an anti-Thatcher pendulum but with a shrinking electoral base. To return to the pragmatic day-to-day extemporization which characterized the later period of Labour's last term of office, when 'blown off course', could be worse than to lose. If it was vital to keep Labour united, the leadership's approach can only be justified by a Labour victory upon well thought-out policies, building upon reality not fantasy. So long as a large and thoughtful section of the electorate cannot cross the gap to Labour and so long as they are reflected in Parliament by a less than enthusiastic Party with a disaffected hundred members among them, then so long will the current malaise endure.

Labour's traditional concern for equality and dignity needs to be rechannelled in the new institutional framework. The Neo-Powellite hostility to Europe, which we endure from certain official spokesman who look over their shoulders nostalgically to the fast-receding past, must end. The basic motivation which has sustained and nourished the Labour movement through this century must be transferred into the more complex world of international corporate power; in this world of intricate class and group relationships the struggle will not be quite as stark as it was to those who were the forerunners of today's Party membership.

Therefore, to pose the malaise of the Party simply as a left-right contest of the old kind is to misunderstand the new forces emerging in all advanced and some less advanced societies in the West. Since his 1964 speech at Scarborough on the technological revolution, Harold Wilson drifted away from those to whom he owed victory that year and, more significantly, in 1966. If that segment of the electorate, now more vital than ever, is not to be pushed into a centre party, or a third force, devoid of socialist content, then the Party leadership will have to rebuild the bridges across the current divide. The question is whether the approach of an election will heal old wounds and create a new impetus in the wake of Labour's mid-term blues.

The so-called gang of three (Williams, Owen and Rodgers) and the National Executive (led by Benn and Heffer) have had their long hot summer but neither side has devoted attention to central issues of political institutions, while Jim Callaghan offered nothing to the debate – the assertion of Parliament as a place that really matters is vital – but, the two factions, however, represent two shrinking élites. At least the former recognizes that Labour commanded only twenty-nine per cent of electoral support in 1979, and also realizes that there are important priorities unmentioned by the traditional left, such as the north-south rift. The far left mistake Government by caucus for Government by democracy. The merit of the debate was to pose some very relevant questions: its weakness was to avoid the fundamental ones. Both sides stopped short of really radical reappraisal of fundamentals but at least there was – is – a debate and without it there can be no new impetus at all. I fervently hope that Michael Foot, as a radical, libertarian, devoted to Parliament and to disarmament if not to Europe, will provide that impetus.

CHAPTER TWO

Motivation

Ever since I can remember, politics and sport were my twin passions. In many ways my partisanship for Manchester United and the Labour Party and the excitement I still derive from the thud of boots on turf is analogous to the thrill I used to derive from an election campaign. However, Westminister itself is often about as dull as Wembley Stadium after a cup final. Visitors are often appalled to see half a dozen members in an otherwise empty chamber talking for the record. One has a sense of anti-climax following the hurley-burley of a campaign.

Since I stopped learning football annuals by heart and stood as the Labour candidate in a mock election in 1950 at school, I had wanted to be a Member of Parliament. Indeed when I collected numbers outside the polling booth in 1945 for Dr. Mabel Tylelcote I was already committed and, on winning my scholarship to Bury Grammar School, I had the heady notion of becoming a cabinet minister if I could not be an international footballer. That year I scored the most goals for the Under-Twelves and still believed that the Soviet Union, which had just helped to defeat the Nazi menace as a friend and ally, was a beacon of hope in a not yet polarized world. Some come to a movement, others are born into it, I belonged to the latter category. Nevertheless my ideas have undergone several important transformations, the most significant of which arose from the coincidence in 1956 of Suez and Hungary which acted as a catalyst to so many new movements and ideas within and without the Labour Party.

As I had a penchant at school for history and English literature it seemed natural that I should follow either an academic career or the law, but in my mind those only would be subsidiary to the world of politics where I believed, like most teenagers, that I might change the world. Suffice it to say, however, that in my formative years sport, politics, theatre and parties, combined with three hours daily hard studying at Manchester University, followed a conventionally happy period as a scholarship boy at a traditional conservative but friendly Direct Grant grammar school. Bury Grammar School had produced a Lord Chief Justice, but when I recruited seven members of the class into the Labour League of Youth and tied with the Tories in the mock elections, it elicited the suggestion by my benevolent old Latin master, a Conservative councillor, that things were not what they used to be. For two Greek lessons, a full hour and a half, we were told how those who criticized Winston Churchill should be tied to a chariot and whipped through the streets as in ancient Rome. The Anglo-Saxon race should rule the world – unfortunately now we needed U.S. help. Jazz was decadent and negroid. In contrast, the lasting influence on my political philosophy was Mr. Hindley, my history master, a Liberal candidate who lost his deposit in 1950 and came into class the next day asking whether anyone had lost anything.

In the tradition of nonconformism and radical liberalism, a powerful factor in the North and in Wales, with an admiration for Cromwell and Gladstone, Mr. Hindley was more radical on foreign affairs than many Labour leaders, while rejecting socialism and Marxism. When I wrote an article called 'Shelley, Poet of Freedom' for the Young Communist paper *Challenge*, he told me that M15 came to enquire about me. I was fifteen and he did not believe in Gestapo methods at school. It coloured my views about the democratic nature of our society. Until the age of seventeen or even nineteen I could well have been classed as a 'fellow traveller' by the less perceptive but I was influenced by Marx and Engels as much as G.D.H. Cole or Robert Owen. The world was simpler then as one lined up in the Cold War and signed peace petitions and thought that Siberia was a capitalist invention.

I had been raised on stories of the hunger marches in which my father participated, and the Spanish Civil War in which my uncle had been killed; and only later did I come into

contact with wholly new and disturbing criticisms of Stalinism
from Trotskyists and Democrats or in George Orwell's *Animal
Farm* and other works, which I read in the sixth form in
school. In the Labour League of Youth (later Young Socialists) and at University, I was to lose my naïve religious
beliefs in the Soviet Union. If they did no more, they undermined my belief in the oft-re-written history of Bolshevism
and paved the way for a gradual understanding of the libertarian stream in socialism in which Mr. Hindley's or John
Stuart Mill's radicalism were to have an increasingly powerful
influence.

What reading and discussion did not achieve the revalua-
tion of Stalin by Khrushchev at the 20th Congress of the
Communist Party of the Soviet Union in 1956 and the subsequent invasion of Hungary completed. I remember being
physically sick upon hearing the news of the execution of
Imre Nagy the Hungarian leader who challenged the Soviet
Empire. It was not merely reading Shaw, Tressel, Laski, Jack
London, or Engels which shaped my views. I also worked in
an office, making decorations for the coronation, selling
wholesale grocery, manufacturing sweets, doing every con-
ceivable job in a local biscuit factory which turned out to be
in my own future Constituency, delivering post and various
other tasks. I learned not only how to work physically, to use
the local phrase 'Scive off' and experience an industrial injury
in overtime, but also how to swear and curse when the ov-
erhead conveyor went too fast, and what it was to have a
little 'hanky-panky' behind the stacks of biscuit tins. I also
travelled, if only in Europe, and widened my vision.

Attending University amid the squalor of Moss Side, as it
then was, the industrial city of Manchester provided the ideal
background. Students were still predominantly Conservative
and the 'red flag' would sometimes be sung if I came in late
to a law students' meeting or lecture.

Suez and Hungary changed everything. Former Liberals
and Tories moved leftwards, like Austin Mitchell, a Liberal
who became Labour M.P. for Grimsby after the death of
Tony Crosland. I first met him on the shop floor of the biscuit
works when he was still a Liberal and I was hooked on

simplistic Marxist economics as interpreted by Emile Burns. He picked up my book and told me that I had been duped, since this was not a real economics textbook. Now he berates Professor David Marquand as a neo-Thatcherite.

Former Communists became disaffected now and a curious bunch of new leftists met at Wortley Hall, amongst whom were Eric Heffer, later to make his mark as a Left wing Labour M.P. on the National Executive, Edward Thompson, later to write the *The Making Of The British Working Class* and become a distinguished academic, and Lawrence Daly who became a leader of the Scottish miners. I did not know then that I would one day work with Eric Heffer on the Industrial Relations Bill; in 1951 he was a member of a forty-strong Party of leftist dissidents, typical of the ferment that arose in those days. The ferment in turn led to a more coherent 'New Left' and, as Secretary of the Manchester Left Club, meeting in Manchester's new 'Left Coffee Bar', I was to meet nearly half the 1964 intake of Labour M.P.s, as well as hearing such key figures in the Labour movement as Anthony Crosland, Anthony Wedgwood Benn, Bill Rogers and Shirley Williams. Also active were Stanley Orme, Edmund Dell and Joel Barnett, later to become Cabinet Ministers. We worked closely with Stanley Orme and also Frank Allaun now on the National Executive, who were the mainstay of the Victory for Socialism group, the forerunner of the Tribune group. David Marquand, who was to leave Parliament in-order to become Chef de Cabinet to Roy Jenkins before taking a Professorship at Salford, was also one of the patrons in the Coffee Bar, as were many future M.P.s, such as Alf Morris, later Minister for Disablement, Arnold Gregory and Norman Atkinson, later Party Treasurer.

The most significant events were the anti-Suez demonstrations where I led 2000 students down Oxford Road, Manchester; the most frightening and memorable was to speak with the great Nye Bevan before 9,000 people at Belle View, Manchester. I also remember staying up all night painting slogans such as 'Eden must Go' and 'Law not War' on banners that we carried following the bombing of Port Said. I can still see the wall of flame as pro-Eden students tried to stop our march to the Manchester Free Trade Hall. More than anything else it was Suez that brought me into the forefront of Manchester politics where, together with my closest friend Brian Holland who came from a traditional Methodist Labour background, we had run the broadly-based Socialist Society at University, rather ignoring the fact that for a long period it was strongly influence by the Communist group within it.

I was to gain experience as Secretary of the Local Labour Party and three years with the Cooperative Union Limited, the Transport House of the Cooperative Movement. Indeed it was the epitome of cosy mediocrity. But I did not realize how in three local election fights in Tory-dominated Prestwich – where I lived and where I worked for such Labour idealists as Norman Proctor, a printer, Cecil Davies, or Jack Griffiths who came from the Welsh valleys to be Chairman of the Manchester Fabian Society – I was serving my apprenticeship for Parliament. I remember Joel Barnett, later to become First Secretary to the Treasury, giving me his Manchester City season ticket to take a night off after weeks of canvassing to elect him as our second local councillor in Prestwich.

As Chairman of the Manchester and District Young Socialists I moved a resolution at the first Young Socialist Conference supporting the policies of the Campaign for Nuclear Disarmament. This was immediately followed by a minor riot which stopped the conference for ten minutes, and I confess that I frightened myself by the hysteria which I conjured up from the interaction of speaker and audience. I marched to Aldermaston with C.N.D. and edited a youth page for *Labours' Northern Voice*. On the eve of the 1959 election I was asked by Alison Kelly, then Alison Brierley and later to be my election agent, to speak at an eve-of-Poll meeting for the Labour candidate for Blackley, Reg Chrimes. The chairman of the meeting, George Halstead, suggested that 'This young man may one day himself be a candidate'. Three years later I was in fact selected as prospective Labour candidate for Blackley. It was my first Selection Conference.

What was the motivation? To me it was a vocation and a way of life. It was a form of religious mission. It was a means of communication. It was also the motivation for life itself beside which my passion for sport, my studies in Law which came fairly easily, going out with my wife whom I met in Paris and proposed to by the Seine, were almost incidental. I was consumed with the missionary zeal of the idealist, having passed through that fundamentalist phase of adolescence where revolutions were still romantic. Life is more complicated now that I have to think out my position on each issue. Indeed choices which had been relatively easy became rather less so with each passing year as I gained knowledge and experience.

And so in 1964, at the age of twenty-six, with a degree and a rapidly expanding junior law practice, I chose to take the path to a lower standard of living but in a vocation I had always desired. Labour had never won in Prestwich until recently and defeat was a condition which I accepted as normal. Only later did I realise that Alison Kelly had asked me to speak in 1959 with the idea in mind that I would be the ideal candidate for 1964.

The selection process in a seat where one is not expected to win is a relatively simple if unsatisfactory affair. All affiliated organizations have a right to nominate a candidate and the executive draws up a short list. It is a hit-and-miss affair with insufficient data or time to assess the various candidates as my own experience demonstrates. Indeed one man who was defeated must ironically thank me for pipping him at the post. Charles Morris, now a Privy Councillor, former P.P.S. to Harold Wilson and Minister of State, was the favourite and shared with me the advantage being a local boy; also he had the additional qualifications of being a popular local councillor and of having middle-of-the-road politics straight down the Party line as a loyalist who never offended anyone.

Blackley had a history of selecting on merit rather than sponsorship and in 1945 the seat had been held briefly for Labour by John Diamond, later First Secretary at the Treasury and Lord Diamond, and by forty-two votes in 1950 before the 1951 defeat. Since then it appeared to have become a fairly safe seat for the Tories with a 4,300 majority in 1959 notwithstanding a one per cent swing to Labour in the

North-West that year. Its councillors were predominately Tory but demographic factors in the form of removals from the centre to the periphery of the city favoured Labour in the long term as did some council house building, so long as apathy could be overcome. Similarly the north-south rift may have much to do with the differential swings that have taken place over two decades. However enthusiasm and organization had to be generated and that is what Alison Kelly and I set out to do.

The hit-and-miss approach of the selection process and the narrow electoral college is illustrated by the selection conference being held before three others in marginal but fairly safe Tory seats to which I was invited. I might never have been selected for Blackley had I had to fight one of the other less winnable and more remote seats if the order been different. Blackley started at the edge of the very street where I had lived all my life. Two of the four wards interviewed me and I had the support of two delegates from the Cooperative Men's Guild because my membership of and interest in the Cooperative Party dating from my employment at the Co-operative Union, caused me to be a regular speaker at their meetings.

At one of these wards, Moston, nine persons turned up and I was defeated five votes to four by a candidate from Oldham committed to the campaign for Democratic Socialism. Another nominee from a different ward was a young schoolmaster who was a member of the National Association of School-masters, antagonizing those who considered the National Union of Teachers as the proper union for schoolmasters. A larger ward meeting at the other end of the Constituency near my home, namely Crumpsall, nominated me and so the three of us, including the man who beat me at Moston, faced Charles Morris, indisputably the favourite.

About forty delegates attended the Selection Conference and a few were from trade unions. In Manchester, trade unions are affiliated to the City rather their Constituency Party and so large trade union delegations were not voting as a block, as in other areas. I never knew the voting figures but the victor of Moston and the schoolmaster apparently gained

minute support and I was to defeat my rival and friend
Charles Morris; the factors were probably no more than
speaking ability on the day, a couple of Cooperative delegates'
votes and the fact that I lived at the very edge of the Constituency. Ironically, within a few weeks Morris's own M.P.,
from the same Union of Post Office Workers in his area, died
and as a result of his selection for the bye-election in the safe
seat of Openshaw, he beat me to the doors of Westminster by
two years, a factor of great importance at a time when Labour
was short of new blood after years in the wilderness.

My speech reflected the position I was to adopt in the
House, which emphasized innovation and idealism, appealing
to the left while looking at varying forms of public ownership,
supporting human rights but not directly aligned to the traditional left which still dominates the thinking of a large section
of the Party.

However, in 1964, the way in which we set about under-
mining a popular local Tory Member was another object
lesson for the aspiring local man who can steadily introduce
and involve himself in local issues – community politics is the
name of the game – while the M.P. is stuck in the division
lobbies and corridors of the House. Basically, the first task is
to make oneself known personally and through the media –
local radio can now play a useful role. My opponent was Eric
Johnson, who had been the M.P. for thirteen years. He was
a sixty-seven-year-old bachelor and he was photographed
with his ninety-three-year-old mother. I deliberately tried to
contrast this with a youthful 'Kennedy image', and a campaign with very many young helpers that was an inspiration
to any candidate, using stickers, loudspeakers, posters, mo-
torcades, and leaflet distributions in order to convince our
own workers that we could win, despite my own doubt.

My task was made easier through personal proximity to
the Constituency. Meanwhile my agent was engaged in the
more mundane but no less important task of organization and
preparation in order to ensure that we pulled in the maximum
vote. In particular, with an October election likely, we were
concerned with new arrivals, removals and new voters. The
former can be impressed by genuine concern; the second

group rarely apply for their postal vote and a visit to new overspill council estates could be an electoral gold mine while new voters are not yet set in their ways.

Both before the election and after publication of each annual Register, a letter would go out to new voters which always included reference to the weekly or fortnightly advice bureau. Other facilities of a social and political nature offered by the Party were included. However, I cannot but re-emphasize that the postal vote was a top priority. One couple on honeymoon in Torquay even canvassed a removal postal vote. A special survey of new voters showed a good deal of indecisiveness and curiosity but a high level of support. Being a young candidate was an advantage but opposition parties, as well as the left, fare better among the youngest voters. Some years later, I was to speak in the House in favour of lowering the voting age from twenty-one to eighteen. Another statistical advantage of concentrating on new voters is that one calls on average on a three-member household. By the same token, each of these new voters would receive a letter and a birthday card. This attention to detail was largely the work of my agent, but such visits and the drafting are the task of the Candidate or M.P.

We espoused local issues. The proposed closure of the Manchester-Bury Railway line was a case in point. I had used it myself for six years. I was to speak in my first adjournment debate on this issue. It gave me the opportunity to address a packed gathering from which would-be participants had to be turned way. It was the biggest meeting we ever held in the area concerned. Only an open air meeting addressed on the eve of Poll by Harold Wilson in 1970 ever drew a larger crowd to the district. This underlined the importance of parochial politics, which affect people's everyday lives.

A leaflet with a picture of a street of terraced houses in Blackley, entitled 'Coronation Street?', was backed by an indictment of Rachmanism in miniature. The extortionate rents and fear of the landlord in this old property preceded the Government's Rent Act just as the cuts proposed for railways under the Beeching proposals were modified sharply.

A curious sociological phenomenon is that these older, less affluent areas housed more Tory and Liberal votes, wherever the houses were just a shade larger than the poorest terraces.

And soon every free night between 1962 and October 1964 I was out on the doorsteps introducing myself. Once I was handed the rent. Another sales-resistant lady started by telling me she did not want to buy anything and after a series of misunderstandings thought my policies were connected with insurance. The most amusing incident was the attractive young blonde who sat me on her couch uncomfortably close to her and told me I was just the man she was waiting for. When she asked me to show her how it was done I looked for the nearest door. It transpired that what she wanted to know was how to vote! Weekends were spent in neighbouring towns and overspill estates, canvassing removals still on the register for postal votes. The local authority housing lists were supplemented by a less legitimate source from a friend in the post office sorting department.

Massed canvassing of the overspill estates yielded three hundred postal votes from former prefab. dwellers. The method was to introduce ourselves as calling on behalf of the Labour Party. Opponents were thanked and ignored; supporters were signed up. I have described this work as a priority and I derived satisfaction from every postal vote being an extra vote. On the other hand, one could canvass a hundred houses and apart from identifying supporters for knocking up on election day and showing the flag, actual converts were rare. The so-called Reading or Mikardo sheets were used with three carbon copies on election day and lists of supporters were progressively crossed off as their numbers came in from out 'number snatchers' outside the polling booth. Each successive wave of 'knockers-up' would therefore avoid those crossed out. The system devised in the famous Reading bye-election is now almost universal in well-organized Constituencies, although something of a mystery to the public.

I wonder if the day will come when telephone canvassing will take over. Certainly it would be too expensive, even if effective, given our strict limit on election expenses. I favour a system of state subsidies for significant political parties. On the other hand, the deposit of £150 is outdated since the free post alone is worth about £3,000 and affords every extremist or eccentric an unjustified subsidy. A subsidy would lessen the power of big business over the Tories and of the Trades Unions over the Labour Party. Perhaps five per cent would be a reasonable threshold (the same figure which permits Parties seats in the German system), or a sliding scale for lost deposits is an interesting alternative. However neither subsidies nor Trade Union sponsorship, but hard work and attention to detail ensured that Blackley was one of the rare examples of Labour obtaining more postal votes than its opponents.

Similarly our window posters outnumbered our opponents ten to one – an indefinable morale booster. Indeed, a motorcade passing these visible signs of support convinced our own faithful of the possibility of victory and the psychological barrier was surmounted. I myself did not believe victory possible until the *Sunday Express* listed Blackley as a seat which could swing to us when many more marginal constituences were omitted. Clearly someone had been doing some homework. David Butler, the psephologist, visited the constituency and told me some time later that he had reached the same conclusion. As the sense of excitement grew, I decided with my agent and committee to put out an extra last-minute card. This emphasized those infamous advertising words like 'new' and 'dynamic', in contrast to the staid image of Eric Johnson and his Party who confidently expected a victory by about a thousand votes until the end. In this at least they differed little from me.

I also concentrated on the churches and clubs. I confess to finding pubs difficult for a pint of ale takes priority over politics, but I had some success at dominoes. Increasingly, I found the ritual visits to old peoples' homes distasteful. A sympathetic matron can deliver a candidate a useful batch of postal votes but there is something immoral and degrading where the homes house senile and sick senior citizens. On the other hand, sheltered housing and those homes where the residents are still mentally agile are quite different and a visit from the Candidate or M.P. is not only a welcome diversion but can assist with various problems. In the same way tennants' associations are a useful source of contact and one picks up a long shopping list of complaints and suggestions to raise with the local authority.

Curiously, I had the support of almost every Anglican, Catholic and Methodist clergyman. Only the local Rabbi openly opposed me to the point of issuing a leaflet for my opponent. However, of the 3,000 members of the faith, the overwhelming majority followed their temporal inclinations. In some ways I felt like a New York politician as I promised to visit Northern Ireland to see the situation at first hand. Our own councillors and activists were a direct reflection of the different communities, rather than reflecting the traditional Tory public school and business image in an area increasingly alienated from the deference vote.

It was not until 1979 that the Tories broke with tradition and selected a local man and a Catholic. Like most local parties, they were basically to the right of Mr. Heath, but were losing their more affluent and educated members to suburbia, a factor which no doubt aided the size of the swing against them. However the ethnic vote, in the shape of Catholics of Irish origin and third and fourth generation Jews or even the nonconformists, has come increasingly to follow their socio-economic position just as they move from Democrat to Republican in the U.S.A. Formerly they were predominantly Labour with a strong Liberal tradition among middle-class Jews which still remains. The variants are still there but social and economic considerations are increasingly paramount.

My greatest boost came in the shape of my daughter Michelle, born four days before the election in a local hospital across the road from the hall where I was busy addressing a public meeting. Bob Edwards M.P., Secretary of the Chemical Workers Union, was our guest speaker. The Constituency included a large I.C.I. complex. The announcement was made by the chairman and I remember nothing of the meeting after that. I shot over the road following my speech and am told that I was so tired that I fell asleep sitting on my wife's bed. A photograph of mother and baby appeared in the

Manchester Evening News. The *Daily Mirror* had published four photos of my then four-year-old son, Howard, helping Father with the election campaign under the caption 'Life with Daddy when Daddy is a Candidate and Mother is expecting'. This was worth more votes than all the political polemics.

I do believe that a human element can be superimposed on our basically two-party and increasingly presidential system as the big personalities and Party leaders are exposed to the media. I learned this in my very first local campaign, when I fought the ward in which I lived against the mayor elect. I faced the anomaly that, at twenty-one, I could stand but as a Y-voter – a system now abolished – I could not vote for myself. Indeed my opponent had mastered the technique and become elected as an Independent with an unassailable majority. Today one can vote on the very day one attains the age of eighteen, but one must be sure to enter one's name for the Register with one's date of birth.

In the event, the result of our frenzied but well-planned campaign was Labour 19,570 (43.6%), Conservative 18,348 (40.8%) Liberal 7,007 (15.6%), a majority of 1,222. Personally I attribute the majority total to our edge on the postal vote and the production of Michelle Alison, whose second name reflected our debt to an extraordinary agent. This represented a swing of 6.1 per cent which was twice the national average. Manchester Blackley and Liverpool Walton were regarded as the two Constituencies to watch. However they both reflected the differential swings, for they should have indicated a good working majority rather than the actual five nationally. The lesson is partly the north-south rift and the population movement from centre to periphery. More seriously, however, it reflected the failure of many marginal seats to organize adequately and project their candidates sufficiently to take advantage of the prevailing mood.

The 1966 Election proved to be almost a rerun except that capital punishment was made such an issue in an hysterical atmosphere ignoring all the evidence, that I asked Lord Gardiner to come to speak from his Olympian height, which he did with devastating clarity. This time I had the advantage

of being in the saddle and the family well known. The slogan
was now 'Keep Paul Rose as Your M.P.'. This time Labour
had an overall majority. I learned that basically people vote
on economic bread-and-butter issues, rather than the emotive
questions of capital punishment or abortion. The figures
speak for themselves: Labour 21,571 (52.4%) Conservative
15,271 (37.1%), Liberal 4,297 (10.4%), a swing of 6.35 per
cent, once again doubling the national average. Blackley had
apparently become a safe Labour seat, if anything is safe in
politics.

Even in the 1970 debacle in a straight fight we kept a 2,599
majority with 53.2 per cent against a tough Tory campaign.
The disbelief on my opponent's face, after having heard over
the radio about Labour seats falling like ninepins, was a
remarkable sight recorded for posterity by the camera. One
similarity was that my wife was pregnant. Harold Wilson had
jokingly suggested in the Division Lobby that if I told him
the prospective date of birth he would fix the election to
coincide. Perhaps if he had waited for Daniel Sean's arrival
he might have remained Prime Minister.

Campaigns are exhilarating. I enjoyed the comradeship,
competitive spirit and the excercise outdoors. There are jokes,
anecdotes and fearsome debates but, on the whole, friendly
greetings for a local boy who has kept hard at work on
detailed problems. I did not enjoy the feeling prior to the
small public meetings in a schoolroom and later tired of
door-to-door canvassing. I preferred my mobile P.A. system
playing music, gathering a crowd of youngsters, distributing
stickers and then assailing the electors with an off-the-cuff
speech with the car strategically positioned at a street corner.

Roy Jenkins, who generously insisted on giving me five
minutes to speak at a big public meeting in Central Manchester in 1970, offered to come to my Constituency for a short
visit the following day. I readily accepted. There was only
one facet of his personality which in a sense illustrated his
ultimate failure in his leadership bid. He kindly invited me
to lunch with him at the prestigious Midland Hotel. I re-
gretfully refused his hospitality. It would have been unthinkable not to eat with my Party workers, whether it was

Kentucky Fried Chicken on a derelict site, or at the local technical college where Leo Kelly, my Agent's husband, was chef. It was Leo who had ferried me to that eve-of-Poll meeting in 1959. Officers should be first over the top and as far as I was concerned I wanted to be with my troops and even more to be one of them.

It was not that Roy Jenkins feared being first over the top as his Common Market stand, his libertarian legislation at the Home Office, and his recent speeches on electoral reform have shown. He was essentially a shy man. That shyness made him appear aloof. I once approached him with the plea to spend more time in the tea room talking to the backbenchers. His reply was as forthright as it was uncharacteristic of most politicians: 'I cannot be what I am not.' The tragedy for me was that good friends like Jock Stallard, M.P., with whom I spent some time in Ireland, could not believe other than that Roy was a snob who would talk to me but not to him. Perhaps this shyness stems from the background of a minor M.P.'s son shipped off to the strangeness of Oxford and with all his talent, brilliant mind and integrity, not being able to put across his radicalism in the matey way one tends to expect among politicians.

By contrast Harold Wilson's uninvited descent upon Blackley did not permit me even a line of political comment, but my proud father took some photographs of his son grinning at the audience as Harold made one of those humorous and confident speeches that unhappily misread the result in 1970. In 1959 Labour had only gained 37.7 per cent of the votes in Blackley and lost by 4,373 so our local morale was not diminished. Indeed we registered the highest percentage ever. After that, elections were much more relaxed affairs and we had a double dose in 1974.

The only difference was the unwelcome intervention of the National Front playing down race but playing up a variety of populist policies. For the first time our supporters experienced having their heads kicked in as they lay on the ground after an ambush. Windows sporting posters were smashed, our paid poster sites vandalized, while crude racism was reserved for close encounters of an unpleasant kind. The

Manchester police took no action in spite of violence and a dossier of complaints, and I could not help telling my supporters outside the Town Hall that if the police would not act, we would. Aerosol sprays and two tough bodyguards for me, a former dabbler in boxing, judicious use of our loudspeaker and our clear determination that the streets of Blackley were not for the heirs of Nazism, made a clear impression on them. However, many voters in that area and at that time had no idea what the Front stood for.

The result was Labour 19,720 (50.8%), Conservative 12,601 (32.5%), Liberal 5,517 (14.2%), N.F. 914 (2.4%). The figures were lower all round, due to slum clearance, but the way was clear for a final fling or for my successor, as by that time my private disillusionment with the House of Commons had set in.

CHAPTER THREE

The Red-Brick Revolution at Westminster

In a sense I was one of the forerunners of a new type of Member, who was to create what I termed the red-brick revolution at Westminster. Into Parliament came a new type of M.P., often more concerned with moral issues rather than the economic preoccupations of their fathers who had joined the hunger marches and made sacrifices to send them to University. Though from the working class, the younger men were not *of* it and were equally at home or out of place in the local Labour Club or the Savoy Hotel. Usually, they had passed the eleven-plus to go to the local grammar school and had graduated from a university in the heart of an industrial city, where they retained their relationship with a class from which in many ways they were alienated and whose prejudices they did not share. The year in which Labour was riding highest was 1966 when a new generation saw it as the Party wedded to technological change. I have since analyzed changes in personnel after my second election in 1966, for that year completed a transformation in the appearance of the Labour Party's representation.

More than half the M.P.s elected to the Labour benches in June 1966 had the advantage of a universtiy education. Oxford supplied forty-eight against Cambridge's twenty-four and ninety-nine products of the red-brick revolution now made up more than a third of the Parliamentary Party. Whereas only twenty-two socialists started life at a public school or service college, this was the background of 189 Conservatives and three out of the six remaining Liberals. The grammar school or technical college is a principal route for the aspiring Labour M.P., while Eton alone turned out sixty Tories and two Liberals, with three Labour heretics for good measure. Liberals were a hundred per cent university products compared to about two-thirds of the Tories (299). The universities provide the overwhelming majority of representatives of all parties and it is the remarkable preponderance of Oxbridge in the Conservative Party, following a public school education, which is the main indication of the difference.

Professionally, the thirty-four barristers and twelve solicitors on the Labour benches compared well in proportion to the fifty-six and eleven respectively who sat for Tory Constituencies. A striking difference was the fifty-six Labour men with academic backgrounds as against a mere seven Tories. But three company directors compared with 107 was the most distinctive difference in delineating the working bias of the parties. For, while the age breakdown of the parties was similar, with Liberals somewhat below the average of forty-five, there were thirty-seven manual workers of whom only twenty were miners; the thirty-four T.U. officials and thirty clerical, technical and engineering workers balance the company directors. Curiously, there were now more wielders of the pen among the Tories, with thirty-five journalists outnumbering the Labour by ten, whereas the wielders of the stethoscope in Labour's ranks – now reduced to a mere six – led the Tories by a short head. The balance was not always thus for the cloth cap and muffler, top army brass and knight of the shire are dwindling in an age of professionalism and meritocracy.

The revolution brought about by the post-war Labour Government, which made open access to the university possible for the miner's son, has now changed the complexion of the Party, where schoolmasters may well be more numerous than manual workers. The process is likely to continue with widening educational opportunity and radical student politics. The demise of Britain's imperial role has brought no less important changes in the power structure of the Conservative Party.

The magic circle which produced Sir Alec Douglas-Home from its top hat becomes a liability in an age when grouse-shooting is considered rather 'square'. The technocratic image of the Wilsonian ascendancy with its appeal to the Kennedy style has been replaced by the cool administrative and allegedly efficient image. The cave men are still with us; the backwoodsmen occasionally emerge from their log mansions but the young Tory of today is as likely to talk the same language as is his Labour counterpart.

As traditional industries such as mining, textiles and railways contract, the white-collar worker and the new technologist appear to bear the prize. Labour won it twice only to see the Tories steal it from under their noses because their more traditional supporters could not be bothered to turn out to vote – even on a glorious summer's day with an extra hour to spare.

Thus, social changes are reflected and exaggerated in House of Commons representation. For a study in depth, the most authoritative sources are the Nuffield projects. The first in 1945 revealed a diversity between the two major parties although ninety-five Labour, twenty-five Conservative and four Liberal M.P.s flatly refused to disclose their educational backgrounds. Nevertheless, ninety-four Labour Members admitted to having only an elementary education and 112 a secondary education. Conversely, on the sparse Conservative benches were 142 ex-public-schoolboys of whom fifty-seven were Old Etonians. Eton has provided the solid core of Conservatives throughout the period as surely as the miners were the solid rock of Labour until the dramatic changes of recent years.

Nevertheless, forty-six Labour M.P.s of 1945 vintage had been through Oxford or Cambridge and fifty-five were the products of the less ancient universities. Corresponding Tory figures were 101 and eighteen. At this time 213 Conservatives faced the solid phalanx of 393 Socialists, strongly class-conscious, singing the Red Flag at the opening of Parliament and never forgiven for the phrase 'We are the masters now'. For 155 of them were 'workers', a status claimed by not a single Tory. Twenty-eight journalists, fifty-four teachers and twenty-seven barristers, together with forty-four professional, men sat on the Labour benches. Only four on each side were drawn from agriculture while thirty-one Labour members were in business. Forty-three barristers and forty-six businessmen formed the bulwark of Conservatism, while Liberals were thinly and evenly spread. The significant factor in 1945 was that one quarter of the House, drawn exclusively from one party, were drawn directly from the ranks of the working class.

By 1951 the parties were more evenly balanced. The main change in the Conservative Party consisted of thirty-two members from the armed services who presumably had remained professional soldiers, while so many ex-officers had dropped their ranks on entering the House on the Labour side. No one today talks of Major Healey as they did of Major Attlee. Seventy-two Conservatives were drawn from the legal profession and 117 businessmen shared benches with 132 directors. The bowler-hatted brigade were back again. Labour's professional element had grown to 103 out of 295, including forty lawyers, forty-eight educationists and nine doctors. Curiously, medical men from a conservative profession tend to enter politics on the Labour side. A solid core of forty miners still retained their safe seats, while fifty-seven Trade Union officials straddled the alliance of manual and professional workers. All too often they were older men sent out to graze, having failed to make the grade in their union. Exceptions such as Nye Bevan or Jim Griffiths only proved the rule. The system of Trade Union sponsorship tended to ossify Labour representation but helped to preserve its affinity with the grass roots.

However, times were changing and by 1955 only forty-four Labour M.P.s had an education limited to the elementary school, while 110 had passed through universities. Out of 344 Conservatives, an astonishing total of seventy-eight Etonians outnumbered thirty-two from Harrow and Winchester. The playing fields of Eton were now the preparation for the battlefield of Westminster. The occupation balance among Conservatives was relatively unchanged while journalism, teaching and the law were the stock Labour professions, easily

combined with Parliamentary duties. Together they account-
ed for ninety-six members, while seventy-seven Tories were
barristers and forty-seven were claimed by the armed services.
Agriculture had also come into its own again with thirty-one
Tory farmers claiming their seats. Post-war necessity had
probably kept these two categories down artificially. More
significantly, the stable element of thirty-four miners among
ninety elected workers was already slipping back as against
those drawn from the professions within the defeated Labour
Party.

In 1964 the pattern of the House of Commons was to
change dramatically with Labour's election to office after
thirteen years in the wilderness. Thus 140 professional men
almost outnumbered 146 Tories. Barristers were outnumbered two to one, but a wide range of professional activity
from medicine to the civil service, swollen by commerce and
industry, produced a new stratum overshadowing the traditional 'workers'.

The process was accelerated by Labour's overwhelming
victory in 1966. The red-brick revolution had triumphed as
103 graduates outnumbered eighty-three from Oxbridge and
together they gave the Government sixteen more university
men than their opponents. All but twenty-six Tory university
products had been at Oxford or Cambridge. Cloth cap and
bowler hat were replaced by red brick and grey stone. Two
hundred and fifty-three Tories had been at public school and
their base had narrowed in educational background, even if
their occupations were more varied. Twenty-four university
lecturers graced Labour's benches, an indication of a new,
higher academic standard entering active Labour politics.
Educators as a whole outnumbered Tory teachers by
seventy-two to four. The thirty-two miners among 109 workers and Trade Unionists were barely holding their own as
their average age was rising. Miners have since diminished
dramatically.

Tories of all groups suffered, but the services fell to nineteen. The age of Empire was being replaced by the age of
meritocracy; no longer bastions of privilege, the universities
were becoming hothouses for discontent. An almost exclu-

sively professional and largely legal membership followed, the only leader with impeccable lineage being Jeremy Thorpe. It took another Celtic fringe – Northern Ireland – to send a merchant seaman and a twenty-one-year-old student to settle scores with the Unionists. Meanwhile, miner's son Roy Jenkins made brilliant speeches in polished prose and in accents indistinguishable from those of a born aristocrat. The Conservative Party had changed little, while Labour's new boys were frequently local lads closely identified with their constituencies.

It would be wrong to try to make a value judgment on this change. It is neither for better nor for worse. It may threaten the cohesion of the traditional alliance with the Trade Union Movement but it is significant that it is precisely among teachers, engineers and skilled technicians that one sees the new note of militancy reflected in the growing Empire of Clive Jenkins's aristocrats of Labour in the A.S.T.M.S. It is an inevitable result of Labour's own educational policies; a more open society with increased mobility within a system that is more class-conscious than any in the world. Meanwhile the articulate young Labour graduate had for a time changed the Party's image and ousted the fundamentalist phrases appropriate to the days of mass unemployment and slump (a word that rings strangely in the ears of those born after 1930). Now we have recessions. Only in rural areas and suburbia was Labour not potentially a Party of Government rather than of protest – a pattern that may have re-emerged in a more dangerous form after the latest defeat of 1979.

For with Labour's red-brick men in power there was nowhere for the new protester to go. The unrest in the universities was another side of the coin in which the populist, law and order, anti-immigration slogans of Enoch Powell found more favour among sections of working-class Labour voters than the liberalism of the new intellectual first-generation middle class. The leaders of yesterday stayed with their people; today they are creamed off, develop new interests and tastes, and even their accents and dress change. The déclassé son of the industrial worker, with a degree in sociology from a red-brick – or grey-stone – universtiy is the typical active

Labour M.P. today. There were exceptions who stand out by their very numerical deficiency and the need to promote as many of them as possible over the heads of their intellectual superiors. But their shop-floor experience may be more valuable to the Party than a double first and a brilliant academic record.

These changes are creating problems for the Labour Party if it is not to become the Party of the eggheads, rejected for its liberal attitudes – as has happened to the Democratic Party in the U.S.A. recently, criticized by reactionary Trade Union leaders for its liberalism. The answer lies in the hands of the Unions themselves. They cannot complain at the new red-brick élite unless they train their best products for a political job and regard it as the equal of advancement within the Union. There is much latent talent and, inevitable as the red-brick revolution may be, counter-revolutions have been known to succeed.

Indeed there seems now to be an 'anti-intellectual' backlash in recent Selection Conferences, often favouring local Councillors, but even the predisposition to select solid Trade Unionists and the fact that they tend to be in safe seats, particularly when sponsored, is matched by a decline in working-class politics at Constituency level that is separating Labour Party activists from the very people they claim to represent. How and why this has happened is less important than how it can be reversed but my own campaign deliberately copied aspects of the kind of image projected by young American campaigners in the wake of the Kennedy era. It is perhaps a recognition of the fact that, while Socialists have a special message on how society should be organized, the aspirations of its natural and potential supporters are to obtain a greater share in the wealth and advantages of the society in which they live rather than to overturn it.

CHAPTER FOUR

A New Boy in the Palace of Westminster

One of the curious features of our electoral law is that it is still grounded in the days when bribery and corruption were as much the rule as the exception. Consequently, as a prospective candidate, one must be careful not to be classified as a Candidate since election expenses will be deemed to run from that date. The secret is to emphasize the Party or the policy rather than the individual. For the sitting Member there is as usual an advantage. He can drive a coach and horses through the restriction by reporting back from Westminster in well-timed leaflets bearing his name and photograph. This is yet another example of an antiquated system of electoral law, to say nothing of the inequity of the system itself.

However the most annoying injunction after the official commencement of a campaign does at least safeguard the Candidate's pocket and sobriety – thou shalt not buy thy voters a pint, not even of Newcastle Brown. By contrast, the moment the result is declared the new member or even the re-elected one will more than make up for his thrift in an expensive orgy of thirst-quenching celebrations after four weeks of footslogging. Noblesse oblige. This is one of the many hidden expenses that M.P.s bear each time they visit their Constituency.

In the Town Hall, the ritual speeches are now public property, although a further speech to those gathered outside the

41

count is usually obligatory. It is one's arrival in London that can be a difficult and possibly traumatic experience for the newly-elected provincial M.P. One is fortified by triumph and the vicarious pride of family, friends, Party faithfuls and colleagues. Letters and telegrams pour in from all quarters of the globe and some P.R. men are already quick off the mark in welcoming the new arrival.

In 1964, M.P.s were paid only £1,750 with no allowances and for me this meant a substantial drop in living standards. Nevertheless, there were not a few green-eyed Labour supporters who thought I had struck a seam of gold. London lodgings had to be paid for, along with telephone calls, telegrams, letters and travel within the Constituency, apart from donations and other Constituency and personal expenses arising from one's new-found eminence. Hardest hit was the active Member. Members with unusually large Constituencies received the same as those which had shrunk - another anomaly of the system. Some M.P.s represented vocal seats or stimulated controversy, while others had passive electors and were content to let sleeping dogs lie, London M.P.s lived at home.

Dr. Michael Winstanley, now in the Lords, represented Cheadle on the Cheshire fringe of South Manchester. Once we found ourselves fogbound at my London flat which I shared with Norman Buchan M.P., a wiry energetic Scots Member whose wife Janie is now a Euro M.P. We had attended a conference on Europe at The Hague. Dr. Winstanley described to me how his Constituency was twice the average size. It was vocal and articulate, being a split mainly between his own Liberal supporters and Tories with Labour a poor third. He himself was active and wrote a column in the local Press as well as appearing on radio and television. Liberals in any event attract correspondence from a wide area because of their under-representation. The result was that he was virtually paying for the privilege of being an M.P. Fortunately, this situation has now changed radically, with reasonable salaries, substantial allowances and free communications.

It was on this same occasion at the Hague that I had

exchanged a word for the only time with Mr. Heath. The latter seemed to use a forced smile as a barrier against real contact with others and appeared devoid of emotion except when lost in his music. Then he assumed a real human dimension that had seemed lacking in an over-intellectualized and seemingly haughty approach to political problems. Nevertheless, his statesmanship showed through on the night he addressed the Oxford Union on Europe, for he was, with all his faults, an essentially civilized if superficially cold personality.

As far as I was concerned finding a flat had been priority number one on my arrival in London and I was fortunate to be located only five minutes from the House with a small office of my own. For a provincial M.P. private enterprise is the sole method of obtaining accommodation. Just as the greater part of office accommodation is squalid or medieval and lacking in privacy, so the provision of accommodation or lack of it is thought of in terms of the gentleman amateur. Some members have desks in corridors in the cloisters. Others share a tiny ill-ventilated room with three colleagues. Others are a considerable distance from the Chamber so that each division bell requires a long trek. Sometimes this proximity with several Members dictating simultaneously to a secretary conjures up the image of the tower of Babel. At least members receive generous secretarial and Constituency allowances now.

The more affluent members can be housed within division-bell distance (six minutes) from the Chamber and can choose to spend their time 'at home' with their own private division bell. My own first office was uncharacteristically luxurious. It was housed across the road from the Palace and one entered from a tunnel by the Westminster underground station. One then climbed into what purported to be a lift but which must have predated the invention of the wheel. When I went on to the front bench I deserted it for the cloisters to be near the Chamber. I have never been able to verify the story that Charles I's death warrant was signed in my room, but it gave one a sense of history and continuity.

The only changes since then were the typewriters and telephones!

My arrival must be fairly typical. I shared bed and breakfast accommodation off the Edgware Road with Harold Walker who was to become a fixture on the employment front bench. He had a capacity for solid hard work and the kind of temperament that can take the strains of Westminster. He would commute to his Doncaster Constituency and home to Ashton, near Manchester, and we were to work together on that curious front-bench team in 1970. Ken Lomas left the House when I did, his health seriously impaired by the hours and the work involved. The contrast was frightening, but I wonder how much it has to do with promotion and the increased job satisfaction of ministerial office. That can only be part of the answer for some people are by nature rebellious backbenchers and settle happily for that role. Perhaps it depends on the individual's perception of himself and the role he seeks to play. Parliament can be a killer for some, while others flourish in the atmosphere.

Eventually the flat at Vanden Court came my way but it had the disadvantage that a few M.P.s and a couple of left-wing journalists would argue politics into the early hours in a masochistic but enthusiastic continuation of the day's work. We rarely relaxed and Norman Buchan and I saw only one show and visited only one cinema in the five years we shared what was essentially an extension of Westminster.

It was not until 1970 that I moved my family down to London when this way of life – sleeping on overnight trains, at airports and in odd Continental hotel rooms and returning to a comfortless flat – was becoming intolerable. One lived like a monk belonging to the Holy Order of the Labour Party. The motto was work, travel and enthusiasm and it was the latter that led me to pace myself too fast for a long-distance runner. It is a lesson for others but one which I learned too late. As the youngest member on our side of the House I felt immortal, until the day came when I received doctor's orders to live in London or leave Parliament.

Life is easier in some respects now for Members but the proliferation of committees, a welcome development in itself, inevitably imposes new burdens. Members are better paid; they have a London allowance, a secretarial allowance and the mileage allowance includes travel within the Constituency. Those new arrivals in 1966 on top of the 1964 intake made one remarkable gain in obtaining a 'family room' at Westminster. This was a boon for younger members but proved equally to be so for older ones. It was a touching sight to see the newly wed M.P. Helene Hayman and her husband in the midnight hours. However, the anti-social hours of Parliament with its all-night sittings was a marriage breaker. The bars were perpetually open and one M.P., who confessed to me that he was an alcoholic, drinking three bottles of whisky a day, suggested that there were as many as eighty Members to a greater or lesser degree in the grip of alcohol.

However flat-sharing had its lighter moments. My own flat frequently resembled a Caledonian Club as Scottish M.P.s poured in to discuss their special interests with Norman Buchan. I certainly became an expert on Nationalism but it was in any event one of my special interests. One Sunday afternoon I was able to drive my wife down to London. This was for a rare sumptuous dinner of the kind that made Nye Bevan term some M.P.s gastronomic pimps. Indeed, as time went by, I made it my business to refuse almost all the invitations to embassy receptions and the like, although initially they were a novelty and occasionally one went beyond small talk and superficiality to cement a friendship and learn a good deal from it.

On that particular night my wife, Eve, was looking particularly ravishing with a fairly revealing decolleté and silver shoes. I dropped her at what I imagined was our empty flat at Vanden Court, before going to park my car at the House of Commons car park. By coincidence Norman had also come down on the Sunday for a special meeting with the Secretary of State for Scotland, Willie Ross, and the Two Scottish law officers. Willie was a tough, dour and straight Minister. He could make an impressive and impassioned speech when it was needed, as on steel nationalization. He had a reputation for being puritanical, if not Calvinistic.

Eve took off her shoes to ease her aching feet and slid

quietly into the flat, only to find herself in the midst of this grim-faced assembly. They were unaware that Norman shared the flat. Mouths fell open and jaws sagged as the assembled dignitaries looked at Norman and clearly thought that this was his 'bit on the side' in London. Norman in turn changed colour to resemble the red flag and stammered, 'This is Paul Rose's wife'. This made matters worse, as they imagined Norman having an affair with another Member's wife. It took a short time for him to recover his composure and for me to keep a reasonably straight face when I could still discern his embarrassment as I entered a few minutes later.

My first impression of the Members' Lobby and therefore of the House was coloured by the sight of ageing Trades Unionists and knights of the shires sitting around in the corners. It was rather like entering a men's club of the kind people join to avoid their wives. The red-brick revolution has now changed all that but there are a few characters in my own Party who make me think of *Room at the Top*. Among the letters I received as a relatively new boy after the 1966 election was one from an old friend from student days who asked me to set out my impressions. It reflected even then the beginnings of my concern at the position of the backbencher after the initial elation, the subsequent feeling of inadequacy amongst so much expertise and finally finding one's niche. It is curious to look at this qualified optimism in the light of the sentiments I express elsewhere in this book. It would perhaps be wrong to accept later cynicism and disillusionment as the total truth, for in a sense both attitudes can be defended according to the subjective state of the commentator. There are some who can play the system and others who are beaten by or reject it.

This is how I saw youth and zeal in the Mother of Parliaments in 1966, after one short and rather exciting term with a tiny majority.

Our first experience as we entered those hallowed corridors of power brought to mind the weight of tradition and ancestor worship upon which Parliament thrives. On every peg where we were to hang our coats was a loop of red tape which we learned was for the purpose of hanging our swords.

The lay-out of the Chamber, seating only two-thirds of the members, with two swords' lengths distance between Government and Opposition front benches, again reflects the days when armed gentlemen of leisure had to be restrained from fighting their personal and political battles with lethal weapons. Today, the spoken word may be mightier than the sword, but the ceremonials that the new member has to endure are more fitted to a leisurely age of gentlemen amateurs . . .

My own first impression was of an atmosphere that might best be described as a cross between a gentlemen's club and a public school. Whatever the class composition of Parliament today, with a Labour Government at the top, the atmosphere is familiar to those who have passed through a university debating society or one of the Inns of Court. The tough, able and articulate Trade Union leader can find himself rendered politically impotent in this artificial atmosphere. It is easier if one arrives young.

But the padded plush of the smokeroom – to me the preserve of High Toryism – was also the room where Nye Bevan held court. True to tradition Nye's spiritual heirs gathered around Michael Foot in a corner of this hostile territory. By contrast the simple tea room is reminiscent of a third grade hotel and tends to be the traditional gathering ground for Labour members.

After all, M.P.s are rather like fish swimming around in a goldfish bowl. Everyone's eyes are upon them and for long periods they are confined to the House. More often than not, their sole function in remaining late at night is to respond to the call of the division bell. This ritual may take up to twenty minutes. Members emerge from all directions, their conditioned reflexes better trained than Pavlov's dogs . . . After six minutes the doors close; a jocular Foreign Secretary brushing shoulders with a raw newcomer and urging him to 'pass down the car please' illustrates the camaraderie that undoubtedly exists among all performers . . . An electronic or telephone system of voting could end the charade, but so far no progress in this direction has been made.

All-night sittings are a strain on the Palace's permanent

staff and harmful to the health and performance of M.P.s. Their justification lies only in the inalienable right of an Opposition to delay legislation which it finds objectionable. The fact that the Government's majority must inevitably guarantee ultimate victory if it chooses to remain intractable, does not inhibit such opposition. However, the Government must keep at least a hundred of its members on the premises, ready to move the closure and a series of guerrilla actions involving a small group of Opposition members each night can keep the House in almost permanent session with little strain on the Opposition. The technique has even been transferred to the small standing committees which debate the committee stage of a bill, thus creating a record in opposing the nationalization of the steel industry . . .

All too often the backbencher feels he is a small and not-too-important cog in an impersonal machine. He sees his function as lobby fodder at Westminster, and as a public relations and welfare officer in his constituency. He sees the Government consulting industrialists, Trade Unionists and economists over prices and incomes before asking the opinions of their own backbenchers. Ill-equipped to deal with the executive, they are provided with neither research officers nor decent office facilities. Most of us can afford only a part-time secretary.

To counteract these frustrations and faced with the immense and growing power of the executive, many Members are turning towards the idea of the committee system. The specialized committee, they argue, would give them power to vet the actions of Ministers and to call for evidence, witnesses and documents. It would restore some power of surveillance to Parliament. Others say this will further devalue the debating Chamber. After all, the Chamber, the party meeting and other forms of expression can still influence decisions.

It can be said, however, that since 1964, with an influx of thoughtful, able and politically tough Members, most of whom were able to command good posts in more remunerative spheres outside Parliament, the strictness of discipline on the Labour side has eroded. Champion of the new liberalism is the Chief Whip himself, John Silkin, who has drawn a number of younger, liberally minded members into the Whips' Office in the recognition that loyalty is something that cannot be forced . . .

And so in spite of the depression that gripped us on arriving at Westminster, after the initial elation of victory, most of us find a modus vivendi that allows us to live with the House and permits the House to contain us. Some of my batch are already in the Cabinet – Peter Shore for one; some like me toil as Parliamentary Private Secretaries. Casualties have been fewer than might have been expected for politicians are nothing if not adaptable. Whether we worked at the coal face or at the Bar, we have been absorbed into the system.

Parliament, however, is having a rough time. Never were there so many active, eager, idealistic and ambitious youngsters – products of the post-1945 revolution in education – in the House than there are today. They are marked out by an ability to work hard and are not afraid to make use of the new means of mass publicity. One Member boasts seventy-five television appearances in less than three years! Having fought their way up from humble backgrounds, they frequently combine intellectual arrogance (and ability) with personal insecurity . . .

But if the House is bending under the burden, it is unlikely to break. Like most English institutions it is conservative and class oriented; it is also flexible and adaptable. A new generation of M.P.s have arrived who are not content to remain as lobby fodder. No doubt Parliament will evolve ways to absorb their energies and their industry, but whether it will in reality grow to curb the growing power of the Executive and the Prime Minister or whether its power will become increasingly illusory, depends on a number of factors, not least of which are the men who are elected to it.

There are signs for the first time in Parliamentary history that there are men dedicated to the principles of Parliamentary democracy who are willing to discard the ritual for the substance; they, more than anyone else, will be responsible for Westminster's renewed vitality and relevance. In an age of modernization it would be ironical if Parliament itself refused to be modernized.

The House of Commons has since adapted in some ways, be it in new offices for a minority of members or the development of the committee system. Also the adversary politics, induced by the electoral system and a Chamber designed to accommodate such a system, has been modified by the entry of new Parties in 1974. Nonetheless, most of the criticisms I levelled at the House still hold good. Youth and zeal, in my instance, slowly gave way to frustration, disillusionment and battle fatigue, not least in those areas where I took a special interest. Governments failed to tackle properly the problems of Northern Ireland, race relations, civil liberties and pseudo-religious cults. It would be wrong to deny the positive role that a backbencher can play, but we should all be concentrating more on the reform of Parliamentary procedure and the electoral system itself and, heresy of heresies, the possible realignment of the radical forces in Britain that this would make possible. The alternative may well be a growing disenchantment with a Labour Party that only assumes power because of the unpopularity of the Government within the confines of an insitutionalized two-party system.

Personally I can trace my disenchantment to Prime Ministerial duplicity on Rhodesia where a pledge that there would be no independence before majority rule was followed by the *Tiger* and *Fearless* conferences. If Ian Smith's supporters had had the sense to accept these terms they would have gained all they wanted. The irony is that they had to give way to precisely that unacceptable formula. When I warned the Government over Northern Ireland, they pinned their faith on the hapless Terence O'Neill because they regarded the issue as too sensitive or their knowledge of Irish history was painfully lacking. I recall Barbara Castle telling me she could understand a young Member getting involved in Vietnam and Rhodesia but not Northern Ireland. More than two thousand deaths later, perhaps she and others understand. Personally I was highly critical of our subservient position to the U.S.A. on Vietnam. Good allies should not fear to criticise. Similarly I defied three-line whips on Rhodesia, which annoyed one Member of my Party who used any pretext to move a critical vote.

A New Boy in the Palace of Westminster

In the light of the settlement in Rhodesia which vindicated my position I well recall my speech to my Constituency Party after opposing the *Tiger* and *Fearless* proposals in which I refused to abandon principles for expediency whatever the majority view. This was a turning-point for me and a matter of principle. It exemplifies the attitude I adopted when criticisms of my actions in the House were made because I had defied the whip.

Thus, through these issues and other problems, like the messy working conditions and the hectic travelling which left little time for home life, the initial glamour with which an aspiring new M.P. views Parliament, is soon tarnished by the experience of reality. Fresh from the triumph and elation of victory at the polls where he is the pivot of activity, the M.P. finds himself a very small fish lost in the goldfish bowl of Parliament. As a jack-of-all-trades at the hustings, he finds that there are specialists in every field. Some Members never adjust to the demands of Parliamentary life.

Others take to the extrovert triviality of Question Time like ducks to water but the majority find their own areas and levels of activity cast in a variety of roles. The initial elation and subsequent depression give way to the excitement and novelty of new stimuli which blot out the essential unreality of the House of Commons.

Members are so often regarded by their Constituents as 'those who run the country' that many of them actually believe it. The truth is that, while Members have a direct line to decision-makers on a host of minor matters affecting individual constituents, it is a rare occasion when a Member is able to influence serious departmental policies.

The increasing power of the Executive and the bureaucracies that so often run Government departments is rapidly devaluing the role of the individual Member. The rigidity of the Party system minimizes the role of individuals and small groups with novel, original and radical ideas. In this atmosphere the cult of mediocrity, propped up by patronage, paves the way for those for whom expediency and conformity are the basic principles of political survival, and the debasement of the currency of politics in the period of the Wilson kitchen cabinet between 1964 and 1970 further diminished the role of the elected Member.

In a system where only two parties hold the reins of power, even the rise of the nationalist groupings has not made many inroads into the immense fields of patronage and power. Quangos, committees, quasi-judicial bodies, as well as the trivia of the honours list and the more serious appointments to the House of Lords are in the hands of the P.M., the Whip, and his selected coterie. Those with power to deflect his course are usually the blinkered but honest fanatics on the more lunatic fringe of politics. The M.P. who retains his individual judgment, intellectual curiosity and the courage to defy the big battalions is by no means a rarity but his influence is curtailed by a variety of factors.

Not only is he a victim of the situation I have described, but he lives in a world so complex and varied that his colleagues will rarely know when he has proven his front bench and their myriad of 'expert' advisers wrong. It is in the nature of the adversary system of Parliamentary politics that, when in doubt on a subject outside one's specialist knowledge, the benefit of the doubt goes to one's Party and its Whips. Thus, many rebellions are snuffed out, not because Members are afraid to defy their Whips, but because the majority of their colleagues are too preoccupied to know what the debate is about. It is this, rather than any fear of the Whips, that makes for conformity.

Parliament comes to life most when there is a free vote on matters of broad concern. In any event, the whipping system no longer consists of disciplinarians threatening the withdrawal of the Whip or suspension from the Party. It depends on a subtle and almost Orwellian system whereby overnight, on the say-so of some unheard voice, patronage is withdrawn and, to all intents and purposes, one ceases to exist other than as a number in a division list. One suddenly becomes an 'unperson'.

Indeed, one of the most wasteful facets of Parliamentary life is the spectacle of six hundred hard-working and, one assumes, intelligent men and women tramping through division lobbies hour after hour, when the majority of those whom they represent have long been tucked up in bed. Some of them have ministerial meetings the same morning. Others have to deal with crises in their Constituencies. Some may even wish to say a rare hello to their wives (or husbands) and children.

Those who consider this activity to be striking a blow for the working class or defending the nation against the militant hordes of marauding revolutionaries are living out their puritanical hang-ups with a self-righteousness that makes saner Members feel guilt-ridden as they quietly murmur 'What a way to run a country' and long for their beds.

The attractions of the Strangers' Bar or extra-mural activities invite one section of this lobby fodder. Others occupy their time in furious activity aimed primarily at preserving their image of themselves as decision-makers and men of influence intact.

Of course, the backbencher has a role. When backbenchers combine to express a widely-felt dissatisfaction with Government policy they can become a formidable force. As a local citizens' advice bureau, confessional and psychiatric outpatients department, they can give full rein to their talents if they combine humanity and compassion with an understanding of legal and governmental processes. However, an experienced secretary can deal with most of these routine matters once the Member has held his surgery.

Perhaps the most frustrating aspect of a Chamber, in which hundreds may compete to catch the Speaker's, eye is the undelivered speech or the unasked question. The more knowing realize the value of the media and angle their activities accordingly.

However, for the caring Member, concerned with real issues, nothing is more suspect to his superiors than his being right before his time. The sheer incomprehension of those capable only of responding to, rather than foreseeing, events, is the same. To be right before one's time is the greatest sin of all.

It did not need a genius to know that the five per cent norm in 1978 was neither acceptable, nor could it be seen to constitute anything like the kind of comprehensive and fair incomes policy which alone will find a response from the public. However, the backbencher was forced to choose between that policy presented from on high and the even more disastrous alternatives of unfettered collective bargaining favoured by Arthur Scargill and the right-wing Thatcherites.

It took ten years for amendments which I moved on the Race Relations Bill to be embodied in a later Act, by which time it was too late. No doubt this experience is mirrored in the frustrations of many backbenchers with far more talent and fortitude, who have to accept the apologies for inaction scripted by anonymous bureaucrats. Indeed, one of the first shocks one receives as a new Member is to read a reply from the new incumbent Minister couched in the same words as those given by the former office-holder from the other Party.

There is still no real power of compulsion accorded to the increasing number of specialist committees. The M.P.'s life is so fragmented and disorganized, his back-up of half a secretary and occasional help on research so inadequate, that he can scarcely compete with the phalanx of specialists trained to deflect the probing eye from the Minister's obvious failures. Our present system favours the disintegration of back-bench opinion into a number of egocentric nuisances who happen to have mastered a topic more successfully than the Minister who brushes away their complaint. Nowhere was this complacency more apparent to me than in the Home Office in the years before I left Parliament.

Specialist committees, not carefully selected by the patronage of Whips but made up of those concerned with particular topics, can now allow Members to build up expertise. Those new committees, with power to question civil servants, to override the idiocy of the current myriad of official secrets often well known to the public, could now reassert the power of Parliament over the Executive if they had mandatory powers.

They can expose and prevent the many scandals that go unexposed because our laws of libel prevent us from writing the truth which may be well known but is difficult for the backbencher to prove. No backbencher without large private means can take on a multi-million-pound empire and survive.

A specialist committee with power to call for testimony and documents can give back to the M.P., and therefore the citizen, the power taken from him by groups in society in many ways more powerful than the Government which should control them.

However, much of the criticism must be levelled at Ministers unwilling to meet new challenges or take on vested interests. Their departments are conditioned to let sleeping dogs lie. They prefer to take the easy course of inaction rather than to act. When their omnipotence is threatened, they can hit back hastily by deporting an investigatory journalist without revealing the cause, or of prosecuting another as if he were a dangerous spy.

Government claims to be open and to take people into its confidence but the reality is greater power in fewer hands, with institutions not answerable to the democratic process accumulating vast wealth and power outside.

Society itself is more varied and sophisticated. The concept of two monolithic classes represented by the two parties is as simplistic as applying Adam Smith's or Karl Marx's analyses of Victorian capitalism to the E.E.C. or C.O.M.E.C.O.N. To regard the present electoral system as sacrosanct and alternatives as heresy is particularly foolish in the light of multiparty democracies which flourish in other parts of Europe and further afield. To a libertarian, the conservatism of Mr. Callaghan or the enlightened Toryism of Mr. Heath is a choice between Tweedledum and Tweedledee.

Our present Parliamentary system stifles individuality and innovation. It is illiberal and based on the flow of power from the top downwards. It is a reflection of the ossification of institutions and attitudes which are responsible for Britain's relative decline. The licensed jester is permitted, but men with ideas and integrity are either smothered in a messy system of group responsibility or blotted out. It is not beyond the wit of commentators to suggest reforms, but it will take more traumatic events before politicians and public have the will to implement them. In spite of this, backbenchers can still use the system as I shall endeavour to show.

CHAPTER FIVE

Short-lived Promotion – Industrial Relations Conflict

My appointment to the front bench, after Labour's defeat in 1970, apart from coming as a surprise, had many of the elements of farce and demonstrates the almost accidental nature of the political process.

Having been a thorn in the side of the Labour Government between 1964 and 1970 – on such subjects as Rhodesia, Vietnam, the Ombudsman, race relations, Northern Ireland, as Chairman of the backbench Home Office Group, and on matters affecting my Constituency – it never occurred to me that I would suddenly find myself part of a team opposing one of the most complex pieces of legislation ever brought before the House of Commons – the Industrial Relations Bill.

The circumstances were curious. I had previously served as Parliamentary Private Secretary to Mrs. Barbara Castle when she did sterling work as Minister of Transport. The role of a P.P.S. and its relevance in limiting the power of backbenchers through strengthening the 'payroll' vote with unpaid assistants bound by greater discipline, is another factor weakening the possibility of backbench revolt. However, I had left that post not only to serve on the Council of Europe but also because I could not accept the penal clauses included in an otherwise very sensible White Paper, *In Place of Strife*, which caused such a remarkable ferment in the Labour Party and the Trade Union Movement. Mrs. Castle, as Minister for Employment in early 1970, was to my mind wrongly cast.

I would have been happier to see her in the Home Office, or covering Education, or Health and Social Security of even Foreign Affairs.

Personally I found the experience of being a P.P.S. to be a cross between an office boy pairing my Minister, a P.R. man for my Minister, but it took me on trips to Bristol docks or Scottish railways. Above all, it gave me an insight into the internal battle which Ministers have to fight for their share of the cake from the Treasury. The tougher and more indispensable the Minister the more likelihood of success even if their priorities are wrong. An excellent Minister of Transport, Barbara Castle should still have realized that each person is caught up in their own rivalry rather than in an overall sensible strategy. Personal pride clouds political judgment on some occasions, as with Christopher Mayhew's demand for an extra aircraft carrier for what he later acknowledged to be an outmoded East of Suez role.

However, Barbara Castle's experience of Trade Union and Party disaffection over *In Place of Strife* was such that she tried to overcompensate to appease the militant left when she was translated into the opposition spokesman on Employment. Perhaps it was because I had abstained on *In Place of Strife*, and that the evidence of the Labour lawyers to the Donovan Commission on Trades Unions was such that it was unacceptable to the Labour movement, that more senior lawyer M.P.s such as Sam Silkin, Q.C. and Peter Archer, Q.C., later to be Attorney and Solicitor Generals respectively, were not invited to shadow the formidable Sir Geoffrey Howe. His long and convoluted replies for the Government constantly made me feel that I was hitting at a sponge.

I always took the view that my own profession of the law was the last to regulate the complex human relations of industry. That is not to say that Trades Unions should be above or outside the law. Some powerful Unions do misuse their power. However the Industrial Relations Bill to be opposed might well have been called 'In place of consultation', for it was shown to be impracticable, unworkable and counter-productive. However, I found myself out of sympathy when the onslaught upon it was on the sole basis that it was a vicious attack on the working class.

In a classic speech, Brian Walden, later to leave Parliament for the media, demonstrated that the values of Government and Opposition were not right or wrong, but different: that the Trade Union Movement had by its history and nature evolved collective rather than individualistic values. The Industrial Relations Bill generated strife, confrontation and bitterness, the legacy of which is still with us today.

I was asked to join Mrs. Castle and the ebullient, pugnacious, likeable left-winger Eric Heffer who, with his endearing vanity, was quick to anger and as quick to forgive and forget. A former carpenter on Liverpool docks with a vast library and deep understanding of Socialist theory and Trade Union practice. Eric, an old colleague from the days of the new left in 1956, was a dissident Marxist shocked at his experiences in the Communist Party. This was a challenge and opportunity I could not resist. Harold Walker, a Manchester engineer schooled in the Trade Union Movement, worked long and hard as a diligent and knowledgable if less colourful or imaginative personality, making up this amazingly diverse although geographically homogeneous team. Perhaps we were all prima donnas in our different ways, and we had heated and hard arguments on tactics if not principle among ourselves on numerous occasions, even during the course of the debates.

We were backed up by a larger team of backbenchers, mainly Trade Unionists, outstanding among whom was Stanley Orme who matched me column inch for column inch in a lighthearted competition in Hansard but with a remarkable identity of views – Stanley as an engineering shop steward and I as a lawyer who had taken a special interest in that field, for my own Father had worked on the shop floor in engineering in Trafford Park. Our viewpoints were convergent and complementary and the blend with capable lawyers like Ronald King Murray Q.C. – greying, gentle, logical and incisive – and the more satirical and humorous John Fraser – a London solicitor who was my successor as P.P.S. to Mrs. Castle, – created a formidable team among a steering Com-

58

mittee that introduced hard-headed diligent new trades union members like John Prescott and moderates like Jimmy Dunn and Walter Harrison, into active participation in organized opposition.

However, my appointment was a curious farce – just as my dismissal was a not unexpected disappointment – and it would be dishonest to pretend otherwise. Not only did Harold Wilson ask me to play this role but he appointed me shadow spokesman on aviation supply under Bill Rodgers, the very antithesis of Mrs. Castle in the ideological battle between *Tribune* and *Socialist Commentary* on the one hand, Victory for Socialism and the Campaign for Democratic Socialism on the other. Balancing acts were the hallmark of Wilsonian tactics.

The argument between protagonists of the European Airbus and the Anglo-U.S. Corporation, the issue of Concorde and the future of aero-space were in themselves of vital importance, not least to me as a member whose Constituency embraced Hawker-Siddeley and Ferranti. I realized that one task was more than enough, but while preferring the more familiar field of Industrial Law and the heat of battle, I wanted to be a frontbencher on equal terms with my colleagues rather than some intermediate animal of indeterminate status. Bill Rodgers agreed that the Industrial Relations Bill was at a more exciting stage and that I should ask to choose full frontbench status in Employment in preference to this split personality but, if I was refused, then he would be happy to have me as his assistant in aviation supply.

At our first frontbench conclave I raised my frontbench dilemma with the team. Unanimously they agreed that I should be on the Employment frontbench and also take over Industrial Training. Barbara marched imperiously before me into Harold Wilson's room, announcing to a slightly startled leader of the Opposition that 'Our Worker's Soviet has decided that Paul should be on the front bench on employment and drop aviation'. Witty as usual Harold replied that 'it sounded more like the politbureau' but immediately and gracefully agreed, recalling a member with a lifetime's experience in the aviation industry to take my place.

Thus was this vital matter settled in the comedy of the

corridors of power. I would not have believed that decisions were made in such a casual way had it not happened like that. Had I thought longer I would have recalled that a few days earlier Harold had asked me quietly in the division lobby to wait by a telephone as he might want me to do a job as the shadow Foreign Office's spokesman. This I would have preferred beyond all. It was not to be, but the off-the-cuff comment that 'Gerald Kaufman tells me that many people would like to see you there' was as surprising as the conclusion I later drew from my dismissal about such kingmakers or creators of petty princedoms. Gerald Kaufman was one of the charmed circle including Frank Judd, Brian O'Malley. John Silkin, Eric Varley, Ken Marks, Charles Morris and later Albert Murray and Roger Stott who were to enjoy the patronage of the Prime Minister. Some, after the appointment of Gerry Fowler as a Minister of State, attributed patronage as much to Marcia Williams, now Lady Falkender, who figured in some scandalous notes circulated by a malicious enemy to naïve backbenchers and duly collected by the Chief Whip.

On an earlier occasion, I arrived at the House on the first day of a term, to look at the correspondence on my secretary's desk. There was a letter from the wife of a Minister accusing him of sexual infidelity, and a photostat air ticket showing where he had been with his 'mistress'.

I have always believed private lives to be sacrosanct so long as they do not interfere with one's job; and such malice placed before me was incomprehensible, although I recalled the close liason between the Minister and girl, who drank together in the bar. Hell may have no fury! but why involve me? I consulted a solicitor M.P. without naming names. His considered advice was to give it to the Chief-Whip and forget the incident. This I did, since otherwise some other vehicle for spreading malicious gossip might have been selected while Chief Whips have a way of killing such things. This was not the last time I was to receive such attempts to discredit Party members, not least a forgery about Ted Short, attributed to a far left group outside the Party, and a forged dossier on my colleagues in an anti-cult group 'Family Action Information and Rescue' (FAIR) which purported to be a photostat of a C.I.A. dossier. At least one M.P. was fool enough to believe it, although it was clearly the work of a pseudo-religious cult.

The method of fighting the Industrial Relations Bill was instructive. Governments have batteries of civil servants, 'experts', researchers and lawyers to advise them. There is little liaison between the Parliamentary Labour Party and Transport House, which seems to serve the Party Executive and work in a vacuum, assisting local Parties but underused by M.P.s. The House of Commons Library serves as the research department for many M.P.s unwilling to or unable to afford to pay for adequate research assistance. It is remarkably efficient but no substitute for a proper system of research facilities. The T.U.C. were not of great assistance to us in fighting a bill which struck at the very heart of the movement.

Two distinguished academics, Professors Wedderburn and Khan Freund, gave us the benefit of their advice along with Peter Pain, Q.C. now a High Court Judge in the field of Industrial Law where the law's intervention is both relevant and acceptable. At least something positive came out of the dialogue of the deaf in the shape of 'Unfair Dismissal' to build on the Redundancy Payments Act which made Industrial Tribunals an innovation. Together with the Employment Protection Act these have now led to the Industrial Appeals Tribunal and the Industrial Division of the High Court itself.

My own views on the Bill we face were set out in many speeches in and outside the House. In the House our Steering Committee together with frontbench meetings, sub-committee meetings to draft hundreds of amendments notwithstanding the guillotine, meant that vast parts of the bill were never debated despite there being 400 divisions during debates which lasted sometimes throughout the night and following morning. The fact that my first major speech from the front bench was delivered at 1.30 am while most members were snatching sleep, sipping a drink or wearily working at their desks is itself another criticism of Parliamentary procedure. Working with Barbara Castle was not easy at the best of times, but her husband, for whom we all had great affection, was dangerously ill. We were all overworked and our back-up was basically our own hard research and practical experience – the latter being an advantage which more than outraged the ranks of civil servants passing messages to their Minister.

In retrospect I believe we made too much of a Custer's Last Stand of the issue and not enough of a strategic regrouping. When it became law the Bill was to defeat itself for precisely the reasons that we had outlined. Its only merit was in opening up debate on vital matters, the new-found collective power of Trade Unions and the rights of workers in cases of unfair dismissal. The rest of it was a straight import from the Taft-Hartley Act and U.S. legislation. At least it caused me to do a crash course, that ought to have earned me a diploma in comparative Industrial Law, and a study in depth of the unsatisfactory and anarchic Judicial decisions that made Labour Law a legal maze of apparently conflicting precedents, which certainly needed legislative rationalisation.

The Minister Robert now Lord Carr was courtesy itself but he was not too well primed on the legal intricacies of the Bill. However the real origins of the bill came from lawyers of the Inns of Court Conservative Association who did not understand, as did Paul Bryan, the Tory spokesman, that the Bill must be acceptable to work.

The Bill was irrelevant and provocative. We want Trade Unionists at work, not in prison, and if ever the Labour Party was justified in its opposition it was by subsequent events with the farcical sight of the 'official Solicitor' getting the Government off its own hook over the dockers rather like the Irish T.G.W.U. members who had to be bailed out of prison by their employers and taken to work by taxi as a result of similar legislation. The real issue is the responsible use of Trade Union power within the framework of a fair incomes policy ensuring prices, profits and dividends.

An interview which I gave to the press sums up many of the issues which concerned us most.

Question: Just how complex do you find the Tory Bill?

Answer: It is one of the most difficult pieces of legislation ever brought before the House.

Q: What are Labour's tactics towards the Bill in Parliament?

A: We are committed to oppose the Bill in its entirety, because although there are one or two acceptable things in it they are embedded in so much that is wrong that the best thing is to scrap the lot and start again.

But since the Bill is likely to go through we can use the debates as an educational exercise to show the quagmire into which industrial relations may fall if legalism is injected into an area which is extremely delicate and complex and depends basically upon human relationships.

With certain groups whose position would be undermined, such as actors and seamen, we must try to safeguard their future. We aim to oppose and expose the Bill. I am against industrial action to defeat it. Such action may be counter – productive.

Q: But what about the Bill that Labour were planning to bring in?

A: Our Bill was positive and established the rights of the workers without bringing in a whole panoply of legalism from America, Australia and Ireland, where the records show that this tends to increase strikes, not reduce them.

Q: Why does Labour's Bill leave more decisions to the Minister, while the Tory one passes so many to the courts?

A: These decisions properly belong to the Minister. The whole history of court decisions in industrial affairs goes against the workers.

This is not because judges are unfair but because by their upbringing and training they are out of touch with the hurley-burley realities of the shop floor. The Tories are proposing a fundamental constitutional change. In effect, they are passing the buck.

The courts would have the most extraordinary powers to deal with such things as cooling-off periods. If the courts are to work within the framework laid down, any case is going to last for weeks.

The introduction of enforcement by courts of law is likely

to damage the voluntary co-operation in industrial relations and I cite the example of the resignation of a
trade union leader like Alf Allen of U.S.D.A.W. from
the Commission on Industrial Relations.

I regard this as a lawyers' paradise and am entirely
opposed to it.

Q: How do you see the Bill in relation to the Donovan
Report?

A: It runs counter to everything the Royal Commission
recommended. In particular, Donovan showed that you
cannot equate the right to join with the right not to join
a union. The right to associate which is laid down in
international conventions is being contravened by the
Bill.

Donovan suggested only one new body, the C.I.R.
(Commission on Industrial Relations) which the Labour
Government set up and which George Woodcock called
the most important development in industrial relations
in his lifetime. It has now virtually been destroyed by
the Tories.

Q: The new Bill would outlaw the closed shop – would
Labour?

A: We defend the right to have a closed shop, but we
recognize the right of conscientious objection. We are
against the free rider who takes the benefits while not
joining a union. The Tory Bill is a free riders' charter,
and the agency shop which is proposed, in which a large
union would be empowered to act for smaller ones, is
the most disruptive thing in the Bill.

Take for example a plant in Bristol where you have
engineers, transport men, electricians, plumbers and
professional workers together.

With only 20 per cent backing one of the unions could
demand a ballot and if it got the votes of 51 per cent of
the work force it could demand to represent all
concerned.

A worker would have two lots of dues to pay simply to
remain in his own union.

The trade unions would be back where they were before

1906, and the non-registered ones back before 1895 – outlawed.

There would probably be fragmentation of bargaining units. In Australia similar legislation led to breakaway unions.

Under this legislation we would have had a national coal strike recently. The rules of the N.U.M. demand a two-third majority vote for such action but under the Bill 51 per cent in favour would have been enough for a strike.

Q: Will you defend the non-unionist who has a conscientious objection both to paying any contribution to a union and to making a donation to a charity which has to be approved by the union?

A: It would be a pretty poor fellow who objected to giving to a charity in return for a pay increase he has been given without any effort on his own part. But this point is largely irrelevant when compared with the big issues on which we have to fight in a limited time.

Q: What about legally-binding agreements between employers and unions?

A: This puts the cart before the horse. Donovan said we must reorganize our bargaining procedures – then it might be possible to have collective bargains which may be legally enforceable.

We object to the presumption that an agreement would be legally enforceable unless stated otherwise, and we utterly oppose the idea that the N.I.R.C. (National Industrial Relations Court) should have power to impose procedures on parties who do not agree. This would inject great bitterness into industrial relations.

Q: The T.U.C. claim that the Bill would silence the voice of dissent among the workers.

A: It would take a lot more than the threat of legal sanctions to do that. But see what it can do. Here is a classic case. Mr. X objects to some new working conditions and says: 'We have got to do something about this.' He is sacked and the boys go on strike.

Under this Bill he can then be brought before the Industrial Tribunal for unfair practices for inducing a breach of contract. If the union regards his action as justifiable and backs the strike it is guilty of 'aiding and abetting.'

This is the first time I have known this phrase to be used in any other law than the criminal law.

Q: What do you think of the compulsory secret ballot?

A: This, from U.S. experience, ties the hands of the union negotiator behind his back at a time when he may just be about to come to an agreement with the employer. It is more likely to lead to strikes than prevent them.

Q: And the compulsary cooling-off period?

A: This becomes the hotting-up period, of course. American experience shows that as soon as a union puts in a pay claim a 'strike psychology' begins to build up. The U.S. Senate Committee on Labour and Public Welfare reported that it frequently becomes a device for bringing to a rapid crisis disputes which might have been solved by patient negotiation.

Q: It is claimed that the Bill incorporates as many checks for employers as for workers. Who gets most, or least from the Bill?

A: The scales are definitely being weighted against the unions. At the same time, I have not spoken at a single meeting yet where an employer has not got up and said: 'We do not want to be saddled with it.' *

Notwithstanding the replies I gave at that time I believe that Labour must not be a mere tool of the Trade Unions. After all, small but powerful Unions can harm large sections of fellow Unionists by selfish action. Not every Trade Dispute is justified particularly where its motives are to resist technological advance or retain unfair craft privileges. But there are organic and historical links that go back to its very origin after the Taff-Vale decision.

The Bill proved to be no help to employers genuinely seeking good industrial relations and real consultation and co-operation. The nub of the issue was expressed by Lord Robens

* BRISTOL EVENING POST – Tuesday, February 9 1971.

on 30 November 1970 when he said: 'On a more practical level it must be agreed that the icy iron precision of the law makes a strange bedfellow for the intricate delicate fabric of industrial relations.'

It could have been – and to some extent was – used by extremists to undermine moderate trade union leaders. It was based on the erroneous assumption that Britain was strike-prone, whereas in the U.S., Australia and Ireland, where there was similar legislation, days lost through stoppages were consistently higher and sometimes ten times as high as in Britain.

However, the anarchic system of collective bargaining, and picket laws relevant to the age of the dray horse in an era of growing interdependency of industry, must make the most fervent defender of Trade Union rights think carefully about the future if vast power is not to lie in the hands of small groups of trade unionists, such as power workers. The voluntary method is the key. Its acceptance will gradually become enshrined in practice, and only then will its embodiment in a legislative framework be acceptable.

The lesson of the ill-fated Bill goes far beyond industrial relations. The House of Commons, just as our Courts of law, are built for and are based on the adversary system. Serried ranks of ashen-faced members trudging dutifully in an outmoded ritual through division lobbies lined with Hansards, is no way to work out harmonious industrial relations, nor is the floor of the house with 630 members the proper place to debate intricate amendments while excluding other important issues at Committee stage. The voting results were as predictable as the arguments. It was a dialogue of the deaf. The Chamber of the House of Commons is rarely the place where decisions are truly made. This again downgrades the role of the backbencher as one of 630 fighting for even a voice at question time or in debate. If there are lessons for industrial relations in this, there are also lessons for the reform of Parliament and its procedure.

There was no attempt to work out solutions to very real problems of trade union power or corporate industrial power. There was no attempt to bring the democratic process to people in their everyday working lives. M.P.s themselves were the 'poor bloody infantry' trying to impress the folks back home with their stamina. Personally I do not believe they were impressed. I rather think that they considered the whole business to be crazy and echoed some of the M.P.s themselves by asking 'what a way to run a country.'

Of course there were some who recalled Henry V and would have cursed the day they were not there; or perhaps they thought of the Tolpuddle Martyrs, believing that they were taking part in an historic battle described by Eric Heffer in the title of his book on *The Class Struggle in Parliament.* It no doubt gave them strength and they genuinely believed on both sides that the electorate was impressed by their hours of vigil, their rhetoric and their days and nights of trench warfare.

By contrast with those hectic hours, on the night of the local elections, I would stand alone at the despatch box flanked by empty benches to left and right, defending a Statutory Instruments on Industrial Training between the traditional hours of ten and eleven thirty or one and a half hours after all other business is completed. S.I.s, the most common form of legislation, can be made the subject of debate although only a small proportion of them (and there may be as many as 4,000) are ever debated. The opposition jeered but what they failed to realize was that every able-bodied Labour M.P. was out canvassing and I was carrying the can. I enjoyed it but, here again, these late night debates which resolve nothing but allow Governments to make substantial changes in the law delegated under existing legislation emphasize the power of the executive and the decline of Parliamentary control. This time as a frontbencher in opposition I was on the other side of our minor fence but the fences are no more justifiable for that.

No real amendments were made to the Industrial Relations Bill and orders (or S.I.s) are by their nature not capable of amendment. If the floor of the House of Commons were not the place where serious Amendments or dialogue were likely to take place then a system of Specialist Committees might be increasingly acceptable so long as they had real powers and were open to public scrutiny and given the spotlight of publicity which is now focused on Question Time. If I learned nothing else before Harold Wilson's dismissal note after I had voted for E.E.C. entry sent me back into limbo it was that I had begun to enjoy the ritual but that that is all it was. Rituals are something we all enjoy but they have little in common with efficiency and frequently block progress towards it. The problem is that most M.P.s begin to accept the ritual all too early and their initial dismay gives way to aimless grumbling without corresponding action.

One further insight into the mind of Harold Wilson came when he called me into his room for three hours before a major speech winding up the debate. I read his speech which was sound, if a little uninspiring. He then asked me if the Treaty of Rome linked to the Industrial Relations Bill would mean that E.E.C. workers could come to Britain and work here without having to join a trade union by reason of the proposals to outlaw the closed shop. I emphasized that, although in strict law free movement of labour was enshrined in the treaty, in practice there were restrictions in that there had to be a job for them. He included a sentence pointing out that if Spain joined the E.E.C. Spanish workers could come to Britain as non-union labour and undercut British unionists. I suggested that to say this was to inject an element of prejudice into the debate. I realized that I had committed lèse majesté. I realized also that these were the first subtle lines in the forthcoming battle over entry into E.E.C., the negotiations for which Harold Wilson himself had set in motion. I knew that for me the writing was on the wall.

CHAPTER SIX

The Constituency Party and the M.P.
Government by Delegate, Representation or Referendum?

The need for a new approach to the organization of politics, both inside Parliament and in the Constituency Parties, was an idea which I shared with a small fraction of members – bascially libertarian and open-minded but mindful also of the new tendencies and greater complexity and stratification of a society which sought honesty rather than expediency in politics. This was difficult to achieve in an atmosphere still dominated by the old divisions between the Campaign for Democratic Socialism and Victory for Socialism, reflected now in the battle lines and serried ranks of the Manifesto and Tribune Groups.

That the Party's view of the role of an M.P. was not shared by the electorate at large was underlined both by a survey I took in the Constituency and by the Referendum on the Common Market – which I opposed – which permitted Harold Wilson to turn full circle in campaigning for the status quo once he was back in office in 1974. Perhaps Wilson, in a Machiavellian way, had achieved two things which he most desired – the preservation of Party unity by opposition and the need to remain in Europe through abdicating political leadership by the use of the referendum, and giving at least the impression of commitment at the 1974 elections in order to rake in some of the anti-Common Market vote. It was with this style of Government that I found myself in passionate conflict.

Our survey showed some interesting results at that vital time, December 1973, when I was most concerned at the Party's inner conflict and lack of credibility. In particular the lack of interest in foreign affairs and Northern Ireland demonstrated also the parochialism of the electorate which was reflected in its attitude to Europe and the E.E.C.

Blackley has always been a marginal constituency with a cross-section of just over half owner-occupiers, about 35 per cent council property, and the balance made up of private tenants, although the proportion of council tenants has since increased.

It followed every Government until 1970 when it stayed Labour after two swings in 1964 and 1966 of twice the national average to Labour. It had previously been regarded as a barometer seat and its local elections reflect its marginal nature with split representation in two out of five wards. Prior to 1945 it also had a Liberal M.P. for a short period, but no Liberal fought in 1970.

For the survey I selected twelve subjects and asked constituents to mark them in order of their priority of interest, awarding points from eleven down to one and dividing the total by the number of completed returns (not everyone completed every section of the questionnaire). The result was:

1 – Prices, cost of living and inflation, 10.3 (placed first by 54 per cent).

2 – Rents, rates and housing, 8.7 (placed first by 16 per cent).

3 – Pensions and social security, 6.6 (placed first by 9 per cent).

4 – Health Services facilities, 5.5 (placed first by 4 per cent).

5 – Industrial Relations and safety, 4.9 (placed first by 5 per cent).

6 – Local constituency issues, 4.5 (placed first by 2 per cent).

7 – Common Market, 4.4 (placed first by 3 per cent).

8 – Education, 3.8 (placed first by 2 per cent).

9 – Public ownership, 2.7 (placed first by 2 per cent).
10 – Race relations, 2.4.
11 – Foreign affairs, 2.3.
12 – Northern Ireland, 2.3.

The high showing of health as against education and the poor showing of the final four subjects, which are all major issues for Government, show the public's emphasis to be on everyday bread-and-butter issues with a stress upon many things that are dealt with at a local level. The cost of living was predictably the major concern as it no doubt still is at present.

Later returns pushed up the rating of industrial relations, which reflected a growing concern in mid-November as against late September and early November, overhauling local issues and the Common Market. A survey taken later could score a significantly higher amount for that issue. Otherwise the pattern remained firm from the first half-dozen replies.

To the question, how a Member of Parliament should vote, not a single reply supported the propositions 'according to his Parliamentary Party Whip' or 'according to his national conference decisions.' This contrasted strongly with the view of activists, who constitute no more than 0.2 per cent but who carry the burden of the local Party's work, of whom nearly four per cent opted for 'the views of the local party'.

Among those who expressed a definite preference, 30 per cent thought that the Member should vote 'according to his own conscience' and 33 per cent 'according to what he considered to be in the national interest' giving a total of 63 per cent in favour of leaving the M.P. to make up his mind, while 33 per cent thought that he should vote according to the wishes of the majority of his constituents.

The problem here is that, without a survey on each issue, it would be difficult for him to do so since most people believe their own view to be the majority view, an attitude which is reinforced by their mixing with like-minded people.

If one includes the answer 'a combination of these' (which is how most independent-minded M.P.s act) the result is:

Party Whip, Nil.
Constituency party, 3 per cent.
Conscience, 22 per cent.
Conference, Nil.
National Interest, 26½ per cent.
Combination of two above issues, 22 per cent.

To the question whether a M.P. should concentrate primarily on local issues, the replies were:
Local issues, 26 per cent.
Regional issues, 7 per cent.
National issues, 29 per cent.
Foreign affairs, Nil.
A balance of these, 38 per cent.

Asked to name the most capable and sincere of Labour's leaders (and leaving out the 'favourite son syndrome' which led some to include their own Member) Harold Wilson headed the list in popular esteem. About 34 per cent of the respondents did not complete this section either through lack of knowledge, or because they considered personalities irrelevant, or thought none of them adequate. Of those who did, however, 69 per cent mentioned Harold Wilson, 57 per cent Roy Jenkins, with Denis Healey and Michael Foot following with 22 per cent and 16 per cent respectively. Benn and Castle scored 11 per cent, and Lever, Callaghan and Hattersley approximately 8 per cent each. First place were shared almost exclusively by Wilson and Jenkins with 54. per cent and 33 per cent respectively, while Healey scored six per cent, despite the fact that Roy Jenkins was not then in the Shadow Cabinet and that he had visited Blackley only once for one hour three years previously.

Having taken the survey, I concluded that an attack on the Government's failure to peg prices, particularly in relation to rents, land, and borrowing rates where they have control, unlike world prices, must be a clear election theme together with the social services and in particular, pensions and health service facilities. Other issues, such as public ownership, would only seem relevant if related to these overriding concerns as, for example, in the taking-over of building land or of the pharmaceutical industry.

The survey also showed the layman's view of party conference decisions, and as M.P.s owe their position to local and
national party organization but are elected by an electorate
with this view of their role, it is clear that M.P.s should, in
the electorate's view, listen more to their constituents as well
as being prepared to stand up for what they believe to be
right when they differ from their party organizations. In the
last analysis they must make their own decisions on these
conflicting loyalties – if they do conflict.

Another feature, is that for a large portion of the electorate,
a Member of Parliament is seen as a local trouble shooter or
ombudsman – 'Super councillor' might be an appropriate
name, since Citizen's Advice Bureau cases and letters are in
the majority, with matters relating to local authority decisions. The fact that almost as many saw the M.P.s job as
concentrating on constituency issues as on national issues –
together with their views on the independence of M.P.s – may
explain much about bye-election successes by the Liberals in
Birmingham, Yardley or Liverpool Edge Hill – the Lincoln
result as well as the Scottish Nationalist win at Govan where
the Labour candidate took the rap for local policy failures,
particularly in housing.

Although I was only a backbencher and had specifically
asked for *leaders'* names, mine came just behind Denis Healey
and ahead of Michael Foot in mentions. The same would no
doubt apply to most active local Members to some degree,
but the whole survey may show that across-the-board party
swings in almost every constituency may diminish in the wake
of 'presidential' style campaigns, and that there may well be
more room for individuality, for M.P.s who are primarily
local representatives rather than potential Ministers. Perhaps
this gives a basis for the view that the Government should
not consist solely of Members of the House, since a Minister
has to do two full-time, and sometimes conflicting jobs.

In my own Constituency the M.P.s dilemma over the
E.E.C. Referendum was overcome by permitting individuals
to campaign as they wished without using the Party machine.
I myself, in a self-denying ordinance, campaigned for a 'Yes'
Vote but not in my own Constituency in an article in the

The Constituency Party and the M.P.

Blackley Guardian and a letter in the *Manchester Evening News*. It was a curious irony that the topic which began my descent from Front Bench prominence to leaving the House altogether started with a principled vote and finished with such a strange compromise in my own Constituency.

The reason lies in the delicate balance between a Member and those who select and work for him. Unless and until we have primary elections, as in the United States, or a different electoral system or a vote of the whole Party, a Member must in part be answerable to his Constituency Party. He has conflicting loyalties and in the last analysis he makes his own decision, however, if he becomes so out of touch with his Party Members on a broad spectrum of topics or acts so arrogantly or foolishly that he is ditched by them that is surely a legitimate risk since *they* select him. One may oppose the present system whereby about fifty to one hundred Constituency Management Committee Members effectively decide the issue of who will form the next Governing Party or opposition – since elections are won and lost in the marginals. One may also regret the selection procedure which is based on a short speech, a few questions and sometimes a pre-organized vote, not least by union delegates. On the other hand, no Member of Parliament would be sitting without the support of his or her Constituency Party and constituents. No one would deny the dilemma I faced myself when I had put my considered view and conscience over Europe before the majority of my local and national parties as well as the Whips. Nevertheless when I faced my Management Committee I told them that they had put me in Parliament and had the absolute right to ask for my resignation. This will be so until we evolve a new selection procedure or system involving a much broader segment of the electorate.

Constituency Parties are not, as a rule, as unreasonable as the press would have us believe. There is adequate machinery to deal with deliberate infiltration, indeed it is moribund parties or rotten boroughs that are a prey to the simple take-over. There is no room for arrogance by those elected; but they also have rights, no more nor less than other voters.

There is, however, one anomaly militating against volun-

75

tary resignation. That anomaly is that, whereas defeat in an election brings a candidate three months' salary, as indeed does redistribution, an M.P. who decides voluntarily not to seek re-election, or is not re-adopted, receives not one penny after years of service. Politics should not be a career; and the struggle for one's ideals demands sacrifice. But the lack of severance pay to non-adopted M.P.s and those seeking to rejoin the rank and file can create real hardship. It encourages a situation where M.P.s disloyal to the movement are encouraged to stand against the party and split the vote if not re-adopted, inhibiting the party's democratic right. I myself, after I resigned, was pestered by dozens of invitations to fight Blackley as a Liberal, or an Independent, or a Radical or any other title, with offers of full financial and organizational backing. It could have earned me £1,700 in three weeks.

One could stand in Cornwall and ask the electors not to vote and pay £150 deposit to earn the same sum of £1,700. The anomaly encourages the has-been and the hack. It discourages local parties from risking a split vote and letting the enemy in. In other words it is an obstacle to the democratic re-selection process. It is time that Parliament tackled the problem.

There is another moral. No M.P. of integrity is fettered by his Constituency Party. He may vote according to his conscience and have the guts to accept the consequences. But the best way to democratize the procedure would be to permit all members or registered Labour supporters to vote on selection or perhaps even adopt the primary election system. The arid debate at the 1979 conference between a reactionary left and a conservative right never considered the radical alternatives to the existing selection by caucus.

The relationship of some M.P.s with their Constituency Parties is one of a remote figure who condescends to attend in his constituency on special occasions. Some constituencies have moribund parties which make few demands and others are fortunate enough to have Parties which endorse their views one hundred per cent. Some Parties defer to the M.P. while confining themselves to humdrum tasks and local matters. My own experience in an active Party, where every ward was marginal and the electoral turn-out high, was different. Its enthusiasm and willingness to work was balanced by a willingness to criticise and it had an Agent whose organizational ability was matched by a hypersensitivity to any criticism of her M.P. however ill-founded. My own oversensitivity to that kind of criticism was a weakness since it led to self-justification where none was needed. 'Qui s'excuse s'accuse'; but my own tendency to hit hard at well-intended or malicious criticism alike caused me unnecessary headaches.

The relationship can best be described as constructive tension. Having set high standards in fighting for the Blackley seat and turning it into a Labour stronghold with the teamwork of Agent, Candidate and Party workers paying remarkable dividends, I underrated my own pull with many uncommitted voters who, unlike the Party, were more appreciative of a naturally rebellious and independent representative. In the 1979 election such voters appear to have numbered some two or three thousand – psephologists tend to underate differential swings and personal following. An M.P. may lose votes for his successor, as did John Stonehouse. On the other hand the Anglesey result in 1979 demonstrated how one M.P. like Cledwyn Hughes could build a great following in a more remote area. But it is easier to lose votes than to gain them.

A Member's advice bureau or surgery on Saturday mornings, tours of housing estates, visits to clubs or garden fêtes and house calls have each more value in terms of votes than a dozen political meetings. It is perhaps unfortunate that many people who could be first-class M.P.s cannot face this mundane but fruitful contact, for one is learning all the time about the real preoccupations of the ordinary elector. This is one reason why my wish to see a fairer, more proportional electoral system is balanced by my belief in the value of the constituency connection in keeping an M.P.s feet firmly on the ground.

How else does one learn about unpaved streets, leaking roofs, threatened redundancies or railway closures and use the machinery of the House of Commons in one of the few areas where the backbencher still has a powerful role as the local ombudsman? Equally one takes the temperature of the Party, even where M.P. baiting may be a favourite sport. One can never please all the Party all the time, but one learns balance. A good M.P. has his fiercely held convictions but should be open to the representations, although not the blackmail, of a constituency organisation.

No M.P. should expect his Party workers to do anything he is not prepared to do himself. Whether chasing removal postal votes, humping sacks of election addresses into the Committee rooms, wiring up the loudspeaker or facing the music at an angry public meeting to back up the local Councillors. Leg work earns more respect than brain work but as the years go by one cannot possibly keep up the same pace. The danger of rushing around like the proverbial blue fly rather than learning the kind of professionalism that teaches one to conserve energy and distinguish between the necessary and unnecessary tasks, is not easily understood by an enthusiastic candidate of twenty-six, elected as his Party's youngest member at 28 in a surprise victory.

Keeping up the original pace and enthusiasm imposes immense strains and destroys personal life. To me the anonymity of a T-shirt and blue jeans in London rather than a collar and tie in Blackley was welcome. Northern Labour stalwarts are highly conservative and less tolerant of eccentricity than Conservatives, particularly in the shires and the metropolis. Even Socialists expect M.P.s to look and act the part while still being one of the boys in the club after a Party meeting. A small local Party social event could render me as nervous as a kitten until I had sunk a couple of pints, while addressing 2,000 people in Strabane with the possibility of a bullet in the head left me composed and invigorated.

The most revealing observation in *The Backbencher and Parliament* is the table which shows that 'the longer a man has been in the House of Commons the lower is his estimate of his own capacity to influence events. Optimism in this regard seems to be a function of inexperience.'

The moral may be that no M.P. should serve more than three Parliaments since his enthusiasm and ardour will be dampened. In fact, the reverse is often the case since those who adjust to disillusion make use of the channels available to them with much greater sophistication than those who favour a headline or a bright supplementary question to the effective behind-the-scenes note or chat. The compulsion to be in the news is not so much because M.P.s are extroverts but because their constituents can judge them not by what is done. Those who sit for such sensitive seats as Blackley are perhaps more aware of this than most; their constituencies are an indication of the altering social composition of the House of Commons.

Conservatives have tended to go on choosing the same sort of people socially, but the rising middle class, represented by the last two Conservative Prime Ministers, have broken into the magic circle of the Salisburys and Homes. Labour M.P.s, by the nature of their position as radicals, tend to be more rebellious but 'those demonstrations which receive considerable press publicity are done because M.P.s want to show those outside Parliament that their view is represented in the Commons and that a gesture has been made . . . rebellions of this kind are often acclaimed in the constituencies, making those involved well known and, for instance, improving their chance of election to the national executive.' * (*The Back-Bencher and Parliament.*)

Such, however, was not the case with Common Market rebels in 1971. Curiously, those who defied the party – fewer of them – when Harold Wilson applied for membership, did not face the same music. This is a curious commentary on intolerance and double-think, just as Tory Suez rebels were treated mercilessly, while the right wing Monday Club excites little opposition from the constituencies.

For the constituent, as for me, it may come as a shock to know that one in five M.P.s holds no advice bureau, or 'surgery', and of the rest the average appears to be about once a month. Similarly more than half of M.P.s are 'carpetbaggers' in the sense of having no previous connection with their constituencies.

* Edited by Dick Leonard, M.P., and Valentine Herman (Macmillan).

Equally, I find my former constituency curiously normal in the distribution of problems, with housing and pensions predominanting. One tip for constituents with strong political views is on the 'Members' Postbag'. The stress on 'quality' rather than quantity is a blow to those who think that petitions or printed cards are influential. Many printed circulars from public relations firms and foreign embassies are not opened at all, and, as one M.P. is alleged to have commented, 'The large waste paper baskets they give us here are the most important tool of our trade. Most blatant propaganda stuff is thrown out.' A well-written letter stating a reasoned point of view is more likely to influence than abuse or blackmail of the threat of withholding a vote.

Most M.P.s enjoy the fight, and victory is often incidental. They will not yield to short-term popularity as easily as the public imagines. If Trollope wrote in his day that: 'It is the highest and most legitimate pride of an Englishman to have the letters M.P. written after his name,' the tycoons and trade union leaders, quite apart from the members of the Government, may well scoff in 1980.

However, an M.P. can try to impose his views on his Party. I did not believe this was wise for, inevitably, those in sympathy with one's approach tend to remain and others join, while some who were out of sympathy would drift away. The marginal nature of Blackley held together disparate elements of left and right; it was part of its strength that it was a cross-section of the community in occupation, religion and local activities, and the biggest split was sometimes between Manchester United and Manchester City supporters, a topic which served to sublimate some of the more latent and serious differences on political topics.

Sometimes, one felt like an American Congressman visiting Catholic, C. of E., Methodist or Jewish functions; while being a welcome guest of the Sikh, Moslem, Hindu and West Indian communities could be a special pleasure because of the diversity and the gratitude they showed for genuine interest. One begins to talk about 'my Pakistanis' or 'my Irish' or 'my vicar or Rabbi' in almost the same proprietary tone as one would discuss 'my engineers' or 'my printers' or 'my pensioners'. The reality, is that only they have the right to talk about 'my M.P.', but Parliament, like a gold fish bowl, breeds egocentricity.

The feedback, however, was invaluable and together with a group of M.P.s including Joan Lestor, Peter Archer Q.C., Frank Judd, Renée Short and local members Ken Marks and Charles Morris, some of us started a 'Talk back' campaign where the audience were the speakers and we responded in our different ways. Local Councillors in one ward took up the same theme and these were perhaps the most valuable means of two-way communication.

Even the 10,000 people visited between 1962 and 1964 were no more than a superficial public relations effort compared to these serious, uninhibited and sometimes rowdy meetings which always ended in applause and appreciation of the fact that we had at least come to listen rather than to preach. I would always try to balance four speakers so as to represent a cross-section of the Party and a true exchange of ideas – carbon copies of myself were the last thing I wanted and the best meetings were frequently with speakers schooled in the Trade Union movement or favouring divergent but not necessarily hostile viewpoints.

The sad thing is that after fifteen years, my decision to leave politics in 1979 was so little understood by my Party that I believe they felt badly let down. They were not to know about the toll on my health and personal life which made my specialist describe me as being in the same condition as a soldier who had been in battle conditions too long. Fighting and usually losing battles had become such a way of life that I only seemed to be alive when in combat. I began to court danger, be it in running out messages for the Greek underground or sabotaging a Mafia boss's car in the Caribbean. I took on vicious enemies who were more dangerous than anything I had met before. Investigations into BOSS proved more amazing than Le Carré spy novels.

I believe that my constituency became in consequence somewhat mundane to me after these experiences. Good friends helped me repair the gap by intensive campaigns on housing estates, in raising local issues and taking me to social events. However, the strain of balancing intensive Constituency work with battles beyond the view of my own Party was increasingly difficult to reconcile as I commuted the 200 miles from Westminister to Manchester up and down the M1 and the M6. One sensitive junior minister once confessed to me that on three occasions he had turned back at the airport before flying to his constituency. I missed only three Advice Bureaux, in fifteen years, once through bereavement, once when my son Daniel was very ill and finally when I myself experienced that same syndrome just before deciding I could take no more of this artificial, self-destructive way of life.

There was, when I entered the House, a well-known M.P. in Manchester, Sir Leslie Lever later Lord Lever of Ardwick, who knew everyone by name, attended a dozen functions a night and shook every hand in sight (even his wife's). He was an astonishing Mayor in the U.S. style. His political contribution to debate at Westminister was negligible. Next door was Konni Zilliacus, author of *I choose Peace*, a remarkable attack on the cold war. He was obsessed with foreign affairs and his views were close to a Titoist line. He flew all over the world and was fluent in a dozen languages. It was said that only if something was more than 1,000 miles from home was he interested. My own view was that one should steer a middle course between these two examples. One should be close to the local churches, hospitals and clubs, while addressing anti-apartheid meetings at the University or founding the Campaign for Democracy in Ulster in Manchester. But it is not easy nor does it allow one to specialize.

If I became increasingly disenchanted with Westminister I learned a lot from the Constituency where I had cycled, played football, worked in the local biscuit factory, delivered post, and where my wife had nursed as a youngster. Even now it hurts too much to go back and the break, if it had to come, had to be as sudden as an amputation. The result was as psychologically traumatic as when a love affair is over.

One criticism of the system is that whereas a management committee of forty make and break policies, select or reject candidates and a dozen members do the same for local councillors, there is no method yet devised of involving the wider membership of the Party. No more than 100 activists seem to matter in a Constituency of nearly 60,000. Out of these a dozen influential personalities dominate. As long as this situation continues the M.P. must owe his political existence to this elite. I cannot help questioning, however, whether the fact that they do the work gives them the sole right to select or reject. It is surely time to find ways of enlisting wider support and participation in decision-making and reappraising the structure of the Party, along other than purely constituency lines.

I believe that the use of community politics will continue with the relative decline of the Labour Party as the natural outlet for constructive protest and concern. My biggest meeting ever was over the closure of the Manchester-Bury railway line.

The experience of the E.E.C. referendum should thereby hold a lesson for the Party elite just as our survey did. The referendum in retrospect may point out some lessons to like-minded elites that reinforce one another's prejudices in all political groups, convincing them that they must speak for everyone and not just for themselves.

An opposition backbencher can rarely influence Government policies and therefore local parties and M.P.s understandably vent their frustrations in internecine quarrels over doctrine. However, as George Strauss pointed out in the *The Backbencher and Parliament*, with Labour in Government the influence of the backbencher on policy is still small. Decisions were made in the secrecy of the Cabinet. Prior consultation with backbenchers is impossible and subsequent rejections politically impracticable.

A referendum devalues even the small influence of the M.P. and in a sense only strengthens those who pose the questions in Government, while giving an illusion of democracy to the rank and file member and the electorate in exercising choice. The answer surely is to strengthen the role of the backbencher, a theme that will recur together with the need to broaden and radicalize the Labour Party in a way which neither the followers of its establishment nor of the fundamentalists have so far understood.

No doubt some people will argue that what justified the referendum was that it relieved M.P.s of their dilemma. Those who most wanted a referendum were crying 'foul' upon the publication of the White Paper, and *Labour Weekly* echoed the sentiment that 'We were robbed by the newspaper and media'. On the other hand, those who strongly opposed the referendum as a pernicious and dangerous precedent were beginning to have second thoughts. Indeed, the relatively low-key campaign with local counting became something of an anti-climax after the sound and fury which the idea of the referendum had generated.

In some countries the referendum has been an instrument of despotism or personal rule. In others, it is a well-entrenched method of consultative or participatory democracy and it is true that, whatever one's misgivings, the decisive result in Britain put an end to a decade and more of uncertainty in a way that nothing else could have done, given the curious history of the period since the Labour Government's application to join the E.E.C.

Nevertheless the instrument remains an unsatisfactory method of ascertaining political view in a system based upon the supremacy of Parliament. The problem is that Parliament decides both the timing and the wording of the question. Timing can be of the essence. It is a matter of speculation what would have been the result of a referendum on hanging the day after the execution of Ruth Ellis as compared with the period following the horrific revelations of the Moors murders. The same is equally true, if less starkly apparent, in relation to the European issue.

M.P.s would have been in an intolerable dilemma if the result had been close, since they must still ultimately decide. It has to be acknowledged too that a predilection for opting in favour of the status quo must have assisted the European cause. Furthermore, it was apparent that the Queen had not, after all, been turned into a President and that the Eurocrats had not annexed Number Ten. Life had gone on much as before and some tangible benefits had emerged from membership. The Conservative Party, which formerly contained and maintained many irreconcilables, had, during the Heath

era, become so identified with Europe that, for most Conservatives, a 'Yes' vote became an act of political
identification.

More serious, as the campaign developed, was the absence
of 'respectable' Conservative sentiment against the E.E.C. A
very passionate, honourable and sincere voice was that of
Neil Marten, but he was almost in splendid isolation as Ted
Heath and William Whitelaw set the tone. Enoch Powell,
shorn of his Midland's power base and increasingly idiosyncratic, lacked credibility as a spokesman for national revival.
The National Front, with a leadership battle within the party,
had so little time and weight that their only value was to
reassure Labour Europeans that, with enemies like that, they
were justified in presenting themselves as the true heirs to the
socialist tradition. Indeed, more than once I heard the sentiment expressed that, with the Communist Party and National Front ranged on the 'No' side – to say nothing of the
I.R.A., Ian Paisley and the Nationalists – even the least
enthusiastic were going to vote 'Yes'.

And by a remarkable and perhaps significant quirk of fate
the ultimate result reflected, almost exactly, the proportions
of voting in Parliament. If anything, the referendum demonstrated that Parliament is more representative than populist
demagogues would have one believe. With all its manifest
faults, it is still a good barometer of the pressures within the
nation.

As the campaign progressed, a rather curious if not altogether unexpected phenomenon became increasingly discern-
ible to those of us speaking around the country. Personalities
were taking over from issues. The battle was becoming one
of goodies and baddies, moderates and extremists. Tony
Wedgwood Benn became 'the man they loved and hated'
while Peter Shore sincerely, but increasingly stridently,
emerged as the most effective champion of an almost chau-
vinist insularity which would have been appropriate to a
different age and climate of opinion. His final appeal for a
community of English-speaking peoples was awesome in its
Churchillian vision but entirely rejected by the grandson of

the war-time leader who, like so many others of his generation, saw Britain's destiny in a Union of European Nations.

It was a sad spectacle to see Barbara Castle out of her
depth at the Oxford Union debate while Michael Foot seemed
less than enthusiastic in his opposition. It was as if they were
reiterating slogans from the age of Adenauer and de Gaulle
when their fears would have been justified. There had been
a time when the left led European sentiment. Some had remained faithful to the concept until 1971 but had capitulated
because of 'Tory terms' or pressures from Trade Unions or
Labour Party interests in the constituencies.

Thus, Reginald Prentice, who had once spoken against a
free vote when in opposition, now joined the European camp
as chief convert at the head of the traditional right of the
Party. Together with the committed Europeans led by Shirley
Williams and Roy Jenkins, they presented a broad appeal to
the electorate.

However, Prentice's hint of coalition politics hardly helped
him or his cause with Party militants, although it warmed the
hearts of many moderates who were tired of the Parliamentary
infighting and backbiting. The spectacle of Roy Jenkins, Ted
Heath and Jeremy Thorpe sharing platforms with remarkable
bonhomie was probably equally harmful to Labour Europeans trying to win over the constituencies, but in terms of
the referendum itself it was a winning team.

My own view is that few reputations were made by the
referendum. Shirley Williams, heading the Labour campaign,
emerged as the most consistent, calm and credible of the
Labour protagonists. Liberals in the suburbs prayed for the
day when Roy Jenkins would be Prime Minister.

Later, in a fit of pique, Judith Hart nearly destroyed herself
after a very useful term as Minister for Overseas Development, while Tony Wedgwood Benn became so much a bo-
geyman that the C.B.I. were able to force the watering-down
of the Industry Bill as he weakened his own authority. During
an intelligent and impressive debate, Benn's remarks about
the 5,000,000 jobs lost to British industry, echoed and exaggerated by Michael Meacher, destroyed his former credibility.
Meanwhile the quietly-spoken Eric Varley remained so silent

that he was able to slip almost unobserved into Benn's industrial shoes.

Like Frank Judd and Gerald Kaufman, Eric Varley had been part of the Kitchen Cabinet that had benefitted from the patronage of the Party leader to a remarkable degree and yet all asserted their independence by defying the Cabinet's non-collective decision on Europe. Conversely, the Ministers of State, Ennals and Fowler, who re-emerged from outside Parliament into these elevated positions, remained faithful. John Silkin, nominally of the Tribune group, was also muted in opposition. All showed their political acuteness and skill, but less in the way of courage and conviction.

The tragedy is that they seemed to demonstrate that honesty and consistency in politics are no longer regarded as admirable traits in the Labour Party. Perhaps, as one of the seven pro-European frontbenchers collectively dismissed without a murmur of protest following the vote on entry, I may be jaundiced in my opinion, but the Common Market issue has weakened and divided the Labour Party, sapping its idealism and energy.

The legacy is that divisiveness in one field is likely to break out more openly in the wake of the Government's economic measures. On Europe it seems that the Party contains some people who still insist on fighting the referendum battle over and over again. As against this the referendum demonstrated that those who shout loudest and arrogate to themselves the right to speak for the majority, are frequently deluding themselves and, in consequence, others.

At the beginning of the campaign Europeans expected a 55–45 victory and anticipated defeat in Scotland and Northern Ireland. Optimistic forecasts were 60–40 but few dared expect the overwhelming 67% that in the event crushed their opponents.

Harold Wilson and Jim Callaghan ran coolly but effectively at the end of the relay giving the race a final impetus as the finishing line approached. The happy coincidence of a favourable Commonwealth conference, superbly stage-managed by Jim Callaghan, destroyed yet another strand of opposition.

Harold rounded up the doubters and a majority of Labour voters clearly followed the Cabinet lead.

A naughty thought then came into my head. Some 80% of the electorate undoubtedly favour a tough but fair incomes policy. A referendum would scuttle Arthur Scargill and the so-called left of the T.U.C. and their viewpoint on incomes policy. The referendum weapon boomeranged over Europe, although it held the Labour Party Conference and Parliamentary Party and Cabinet together. It could yet be used to quell an incipient revolt from the far left. Its enthusiastic supporters may regret the day that Benn's brainchild was adopted by the Labour Party Manifesto.

CHAPTER SEVEN

The Member's Positive Role

Notwithstanding all my criticisms, Members do have a role in Parliament and there are methods by which tenacious backbenchers can make inroads into executive power. It is these avenues and the platform which membership gives for airing views and organizing campaigns that justifies the honest Member in remaining to fight.

The first and most obvious channel of communication is the least visible to the onlooker or the media. This is the direct contact the Member has with Ministers and others in the lobbies, the bar or the tea room, or even through the post. Indeed a letter from a M.P. can sometimes set bureaucrats in Town Halls and Government Offices into a something of a panic.

If there is one area of satisfaction which I had it was in playing the role of local ombudsman, but that is hardly the role M.P.s are elected to play. There was a high rate of success on individual cases from the Constituency. The real Ombudsman is relevant to few cases, however, and while I took an active part on the committee stage of the Bill which set up this institution I found his role so limited that I did not refer a single case to him.

This local work sometimes dominated my activities. The overwhelming majority of my cases in an urban constituency concerned housing. A never-ending stream of missives seemed to pass between me and the Director of Housing in the Manchester Town Hall. Adverse publicity was the ultimate weapon. Ironically all this should properly have been dealt with by local Councillors and often constituents tried both local and national channels of appeal.

Social security and tax cases, on the other hand, fell within the province of National Government as did Home Office matters such as immigration. I deplored the habit of immigration officials in detaining bona fide visitors and students at airports on Friday night or even Christmas day when they no doubt thought no M.P. would easily be found. As a consequence I became particularly involved since no one is deported while a Member is pursuing the case.

A M.P. has to be a marriage guidance counsellor, even if his anti-social hours are breaking up his own marriage. He has to be a legal adviser even if he has little experience of the workings of the law. There, I found my profession to be a great advantage. He has to receive delegations even if public relations are not his strongpoint. However, the very fact of being a Member turns one into an unofficial P.R. man. Of all the lobbies I had to contend with the most persistent and vocal was the anti-abortion lobby. I had voted for David Steele's Bill and while I believe this is a matter where only a woman can decide for herself, I confess to finding the topic one which caused more of an internal battle with my conscience than any other, perhaps because of the way in which pro-abortionists dismissed their opponents' arguments. Similarly, the opponents antagonized me with phrases such as 'murder'. The result was that each delegation proved counter-productive because of its extremism. Sometimes I seemed to be no more than a receiver of deputations and go-between on local matters. They ranged from the threatened closure of a much-loved public house to the threatened destruction of a golf course. I still have a tie to show for the latter campaign, although the course now houses a large group of suburban dwellings.

The stream of 'thank-you' letters and the old ladies who literally cried on my shoulder helped sustain me through difficult times. My criticism is, however, that a reasonably trained and sympathetic social worker could do most of this work adequately. It is a sad commentary on community services and local Councils that a so-called legislator spends a major part of his time writing to local authorities asking for Council House transfers and repairs, or new street lamps and bus shelters. My last secretary, Maggie Harrison, could deal with the housing matters once I had processed them. Having served the two airport M.P.s, Russell Kerr and Neville Sandleson, she was more of an expert on tackling the Home Office on immigration matters than I ever became.

The next method of getting over a point, collecting information, or just keeping in the public eye is Question Time. Although it tends to be monopolized by exhibitionists and self-publicists, it still provides a method of focussing public attention on important issues or collecting information for use in debate at a later time. For the latter purpose the written question is frequently more effective in eliciting a detailed reply. Frequently the very fact of tabling a question permits the media to expand on the story. Newspaper quotes or radio and T.V. interviews often follow and permit the expression of a strongly held viewpoint to an audience of millions.

I recall at ten minutes to six one evening being on tenterhooks waiting to speak on the Race Relations Bill second reading, knowing that a cab was to pick me up at 6 p.m. for a T.V. interview. I mentioned my dilemma to Brian Walden. He looked at me in astonishment. In the Chamber I would be heard by a dozen or two Members basically interested in their own as yet undelivered speeches. Outside was an audience of millions. My words might receive a few lines in the quality press and a sentence in *Today in Parliament*. Significantly Brian Walden now has his own programme interviewing prominent politicians and has been true to his priorities. Fortunately my dilemma was resolved. At that moment the Speaker called me and I said what I had to say in ten minutes flat, a discipline now imposed on Members.

The problem with Question Time, apart from its length, is that no Minister need really answer the question. Some rarely do. It is certainly not Answer Time, and the hour often becomes a vehicle for Party points to be scored through contrived questions. One merely uses the formula 'Is the Minister aware that?' before making one's statement. Often questions are fed to Ministers by their own supporters. The planted question is usually channelled through the Minister's Parliamentary Private Secretary. It cuts down the number of hostile questions called. It gives the Minister a chance to tell success stories. As P.P.S. to Barbara Castle at the Transport Ministry I became adept at selecting twenty colleagues for this legitimate but discreditable task. We even held a meeting of Ministers to select these public relations gifts before distributing them among the Party faithful.

With the new breed of Members there is a strict limit on oral questions. Nevertheless the number of questions continues to rise and one wonders whether they should be limited. This would curtail one of the most valuable ways of prodding the Executive and the limit should only apply to oral questions to preserve fairness. Some statistics on Members' questions omit the supplementaries. Wise M.P.s often wait for someone else's question to be answered and then rise on a supplementary. The risk is that one is not called or that the original questioner fails to appear to ask his question. Sometimes I found a tendency, apart from priority for Privy Councillors and Opposition Front Bench Spokesman, for Speaker George Thomas to call the same contributors. Some Members deliberately try to make the Speaker's life difficult. It is no wonder that they and their aides tend to notice the faces with which they are already most familiar.

I remember that when Mr. Selwyn Lloyd was Speaker I rose twenty-eight times without being called. When I drew his attention to this he could not have been kinder, and I was almost embarrassed thereafter at the way I was called early in debates. What annoyed me was that self-restraint in intervening would not ensure being called. Some people seemed to have a prescriptive right to opine on any topic.

The new rota system has proved more fair but it is offset by longer periods on supplementaries so that only twenty or so questions will be reached in any one day. The number has shrunk since 1964. What occurs is a sort of lively mini-debate, but since the Minister can be questioned only every few weeks one has to be obsessional in order to get at him. The question has to be delivered to the table office exactly two weeks ahead, I found the whole procedure increasingly irritating, with its lack of spontaneity. One Member who lost his seat, only to replace a notorious ex-Member, was sometimes referred to as 'Ask a Question', so predictable was his contribution. A busy and serious M.P. is unlikely to succeed more than on infrequent occasions in eliciting a meaningful response to an oral question. To quote *The Commons in the Seventies* (Walkland and Ryle):

> 'Let us suppose that by perseverence and foresight on the part of a Member his question is eventually reached and he is not satisfied with the reply. Unlike the Member of fifty or sixty years ago he knows that if he lets his chance slip he may not reach the Minister for another four or five weeks.'

This is a far cry from Erskine May's comment in 1861 that the practice had greatly increased during the last ten years but it was exercised with comparative rarity and in no cases were the notices printed.

If the questions were still a novelty in the 1860s there is little doubt about the unsatisfactory nature of Question Time by the 1960s. Occasionally one can make a telling point. Now and again a Minister is left groggy on the ropes, but is never counted out. There are questions without Party advantage that receive genuine replies. Skilful Members can bowl googlies but a clever Minister plays a straight bat. The witty or thoughtful supplementary question is the best way to catch a Minister napping but the advantage always lies with the man standing at the Despatch Box, his book open with prepared responses to the permutation of possible supplementaries and a caucus of civil servants to back him up.

The scope for questioning the Prime Minister has narrowed. Too many questions are transferred to other Ministers. The technique is to ask the P.M. to announce his or her engagements for April 1st or whether he or she will visit Neasden. This then permits a supplementary on a variety of topics. The fifteen minutes at 3.15 p.m. on Tuesday and Thursday are the most publicized and well attended events of the Parliamentary week. Certain Members glory in the occasion, but as a vehicle for obtaining information it is largely irrelevant. It has all the attraction of a tough cup tie. Indeed, if I have used metaphors from three sports, the whole process does indeed have a lot in common with boxing, cricket and soccer, although it sometimes degenerates into a rugby scrum. That, of course, is in the nature of the basically two-party adversary system.

The Private Notice Question is another matter for the discretion of the Speaker and the Minister. It is an important way of raising an urgent and important topic or event. Like all other questions it is all too easy for the Minister to side-step the issue on the basis of insufficient knowledge precisely because the question is about something very topical. Again the answer may be a string of pious platitudes while the Government stalls in order to decide what action, if any, to take. Members anxious to obtain the maximum statistical information will do best to put down a written question. Question Time and more particularly Prime Minister's Question Time are undoubtedly the hour of the extrovert.

As a newly initiated questioner I formed the view that there should be a rationing system for Question Time. I wanted to curb the exuberance and concentrate the minds of that small group of members who seemed to dominate it. Over the last eighty years the functions of Ministers have multipled the area of questioning by as much as thirty. The number of questions receiving oral replies has diminished by two-thirds. The modern Member therefore has only a 1½% of satisfaction as against his Victorian or Edwardian counterpart.

The mechanics of questioning are not often explained to the outsider. The Member takes or sends his question written out to the Table Office. Frequently it has to be amended to be in order. It is then printed on the Order Paper for the date chosen. A bunch is received before selecting the order. Otherwise Members would queue up. The Order Paper is the Programme of the Match for the day. The Member states the number and after the reply he can then ask a supplementary. One backbencher who did not waste words was Tam Dalyell who often stumbled on remarkably esoteric scandals. He once showed how a backbencher could expose a Minister with the simple word 'Why?'

Even if the backbenchers' privilege of questioning the Executive has lost much of it effectiveness, it is still the liveliest time of most days. Too often the average Member is reduced to the role of a spectator on the terraces, cheering on rival frontbenchers as they deftly try to penetrate the defences of the Minister. The layout of Parliament and the sheer size of membership reduces the possibility of questioning and speaking so that other channels may be more attractive.

This was one of the strong arguments for specialist committees and regional devolution. Assemblies which coincided with existing Government regional offices rather than the present mix of Scottish and Welsh Government or counties and metropolitan boroughs would also relieve the burden while spreading power. Instruments which were innovations in the days of the gentleman amateur are no longer relevant today. Government has grown twenty-five times over but the House remains much as it was in the days of Gladstone and Disraeli.

Question Time nonetheless has its value. Merely getting the question down on the Order Paper may be enough to alert public opinion even though as a vehicle for obtaining information it is inadequate. It is all the more remarkable, therefore, that many Members have become so skilful that they can seriously embarrass Ministers. They may even make the Minister go away and rethink his intentions or start a mini-debate, the consequencies of which may on occasion cause ripples to widen into a public controversy.

If Question Time is unsatisfactory, the backbencher may fall back on the lonely but in some ways satisfying weapon of the daily adjournment debate. This completes each day, however long, with thirty minutes devoted to one backbencher's preoccupation. This may well be of purely local interest. Parliamentary sessions end with one whole day of longer adjournment debates that resemble mini Private Members' motions. After researching a topic thoroughly and exhausting written and oral questions, I found the adjournment debate a valuable means of airing constituency and broader grievances.

Questions on these occasions are especially useful, supplying data provided by (and therefore undeniable by) the Government itself. Unlike the short questions they allow one time to develop a coherent argument. Sometimes I would order copies to use as one would use a pamphlet, making sure of obtaining good coverage in the local press for items of local or regional interest. The disadvantage of adjournment debates is that one may speak eloquently to an empty chamber at an unearthly hour of the morning. The fruits of this lonely vigil may be too late for the Daily Press and go unnoticed among Parliamentarians and public alike.

The range of topic raised may be gleaned from my own personal list. For me it was often the final stage of grievance procedure or part of a campaign. The debates are selected by ballot although the Speaker may select one each week. Luck therefore plays a major part but perseverance is necessary. It was during my adjournment debate on Race Relations that the National Executive Member Joan Lestor made her maiden speech before Christmas 1966. By the same token I was able to speak on Rhodesia in a debate introduced early on by Stan Newens when the rest of the day's business finished early. Thus we had several hours until half past ten – the normal early closing time of the House of Commons.

The following list of the major adjournment debates, Private Members' motions and other methods of raising one's interests says something about the diversity of Parliamentary life but I suspect it may say more about me.

Transport: Closure of the Manchester-Bury Railway line
Aviation: The case for building the H.S. 146
Employment: The economic problems of the North West
Environment: The conservation of Crab Lane, Blackley
The preservation of Failsworth Golf Course, Blackley
Safety in children's playgrounds
Manchester housing (Charles Morris's debate)
Home Office: Race relations
The Unification Church
Civil liberties
Health and Social Security: Industrial diseases not qualifying for benefit
Unification Church

Closure of a local hospital's accident unit
The needs of autistic children
Foreign Affairs: Rhodesia (Stan Newen's debate)
The other procedures for raising such subjects include Standing Order No. 9, Private Bills and motions, certain local orders, and the Consolidated Fund Bill which is usually a marathon sitting on which just about everything may be raised.

My one S.O.9 was on Northern Ireland when Bernadette Devlin made her maiden speech. Orders let me take up pet topics such as the Park Forest and Lancaster Canals from a conservationist viewpoint. Private Members permitted me to air my views on industrial safety (Neil Kinnock's debate) and sports facilities (John Hunt). Indeed John Hunt's debate probably led to my appointment by Denis Howell, Minister for Sport, as Chairman of the North West Sports Council just before the 1966 Election. This little bit of patronage meant hard work in getting the Council off the ground, but with it went some perks such as a seat in the Directors' box at Old Trafford, Goodison Park and Wembley: Brazil v. Hungary was one of the most memorable matches I saw. Ultimately, however – and perhaps this is a facet of my own character – I resigned when I felt I had got the wheels moving and I was beginning to repeat myself. I had admittedly also become a P.P.S., but the Councils had no finance of their own to distribute and were in danger of degenerating into talking shops.

On an earlier occasion I delivered a long filibustering speech on consumer protection made in the middle of the night on the Consolidated Fund Bill. In those days I was not schooled in checking the Hansard reporters, who seem less able or more tired at night, but their errors were better than the speech, with 'gloved hand' coming out as 'bloodhound'.

Indeed, Health, Transport, Environment and Education, followed by the Home Office, tend to be the main targets for these debates. They lack the excitement of Question Time, but they give a rare opportunity to develop a case thoroughly on a matter chosen by the Private Member rather than the usual channels – the Whips, Government and what are known as Opposition supply days. They allow members to spotlight grievances that may well be local, although this by no means rules out matters of national concern.

The other methods include Standing Order No. 9 which is used sparingly on a very urgent matter. Notice is given to the Speaker and forty members have to rise in support to permit a three-hour debate the following day. The Speaker's decision is final. I was able to use this only once and that is once more than many members. I flew down to London on a Monday morning and with 45 minutes to go to the end of Question Time, the taxi driver rushed the rest of the way to the House. I was able to obtain a debate on Northern Ireland following the eruption of violence. This was an achievement, after years of procedural blockages on the topic. It was on this occasion that, after numerous telephone calls, cajoling and persuasion, not least by Gerry Fitt, Bernadette Devlin came to West-minster. The sole representative of the minority, she was regarded as a child prodigy and surrounded by an exclusive entourage that was hostile to her well-wishers, she neverthe-less dined with the Labour Whips, John Silkin and Brian O'Malley and her sponsors, Gerry and myself.

I opened the debate but this was really Bernadette's day as she made a brilliantly destructive maiden speech that con-tained no positive proposals. The irony was that for a time she was the only member of the House with whom I was not on speaking terms. Simultaneously I was attacked for spon-soring her. In politics one cannot win! She arrogated to herself the sole right to speak on behalf of the people of Ireland although espousing an extreme view that reflected one of the Trotskyist groups that undoubtedly influenced her. This re-sulted in divisions among those of us who championed the cause of civil rights. Barbara Castle was constrained to sug-gest that I should use unorthodox ways of shutting up Ber-nadette, adding that 'We all have to make sacrifices for the cause.'

After 'Bloody Sunday' Bernadette slapped Mr. Maudling's face. Without condoning that action, I feel it is a pity that there are not more such difficult members who have no regard for the hallowed traditions of the House. In fact, most Private Members' motions and debates tend to be friendly and intimate affairs with less feeling of Party loyalty. Some Bills, such as David Steel's Termination of Pregnancy Bill, can generate very deep and strong emotions.

Such debates and Bills are selected by ballot which can be a little unfair on those who are never drawn. Once I had a number two and three on a Friday which were never reached! However, with the exception of education and the inclusion of special interests such as Northern Ireland and cults, my own list is a reasonable reflection of the kind of topics that are raised. The vast numbers of former teachers and lecturers on the Labour Benches was such that I felt inhibited about speaking on this over-popular area. Sometimes the very fact that one is drawn out of the hat can provoke wide interest among the media, rather like tabling an unreached question.

One problem facing a crusading M.P. is that the media will consult him on a topic repeatedly so that the public identify him solely with that one issue. An M.P. may have spent months in battle on behalf of his constituents as well as several major issues. He is then the subject of recrimination for concentrating solely on the topic with which the media have identified him.

The only consolation in being drawn too late to be heard is that the very wording of a motion may provoke intense interest. I have now amassed a collection of books on Ireland and written two myself as my interest increased. Between 1965 and 1969 this became a major part of my work although unconnected with my Constituency. It provoked adulation on the one hand and hatred on the other. It was only when the *Sunday Times* and *The Observer* published feature articles that we began to break through the wall of silence that equally afflicted me when I became involved in a battle against a powerful pseudo-religious cult. If M.P.s do not crusade on what may at first appear to be esoteric topics then their role can be severely limited.

The other topic drawn out was on the danger of much of the equipment in Children's playgrounds. It received scant notice until I again raised it at Question Time with a moderately good response and used my information for an adjournment debate. Nothing should ever be wasted. It brought me into contact with the organization Fair Play For Children. The daily toll of injuries and damaged limbs was apparently not sensational enough for those who sought eye-catching headlines.

There is a curious interaction between drawing attention to topics in Parliament and the receipt of further information that allows one to build up a useful file. The press and television or radio may bite, and even documentaries may follow. Letters may pour in, sometimes containing cuttings. Some arrive from Australia and New Zealand or the United States. The process may be cumulative, but however one's expertise grows, the pious palliatives or scepticism of Ministers may dampen one's ardour. Even when one is successful one wonders whether one's contribution has added to the weight in the scales of decision-making. At least one receives some public acclaim from such lobbies as those for Crab Lane or the H.S.146 aircraft, but one suspects that the decisions are not motivated by any desire to placate the mover of the motion.

The Consolidated Fund debate is so wide that it resembles a series of adjournment debates lasting through the day and night. It is a rather masochistic exercise requiring patience and stamina beyond the normal call of duty. I began to feel a true Parliamentarian after my own contribution on Consumer Protection. Our object was to keep the debate going so long that the next day's business would be lost. We succeeded, but in retrospect it was a shabby manoevre at a time when loyalty to the antics of the Whips' office was not yet a thing of the past. In those days an opportunity to prove one's worth to the Party was not to be scorned. The following day's Bill to be introduced by the late Airey Neave would have removed the anomaly which denied pension rights to the very old and even if the Tories were hypocritical in doing the same, that was no excuse for not being honest about it on opposing the Bill or doing the right thing in supporting it.

The fact that, after a few weeks in 1964, Labour's proposals for increased social security benefits had caused a run on the pound, made us fear the gnomes of Zurich. Indeed the lack of real independence at Westminster on economic and foreign affairs was a humiliating revelation. It was a major factor in my conversion to the E.E.C. as it was with Michael Barnes, Professor John Mackintosh and others who saw that Britain could no longer stand alone, however critical we might be of the Common Agricultural Policy.

Parliamentary manoeuvring may seem childish. I had a particular aversion to Ministers throwing about quotations from previous Governments in justifying their stance. It did not make it right or wrong, which was surely the real issue. Such double standards are a feature of the ins and outs of confrontation politics which we uphold on the basis of a tiny percentage swing in public opinion on one day. Blind loyalty to the Whips or antipathy to the other side is often a more powerful motivating force than the arguments deployed or the cogency of a case.

I regret that I never came out of the hat for Private Members Bills. It can be the making of a reputation. It also is one of the areas where a backbencher can actually change some aspect of the nation's life. Some, like Leo Abse, really use their position effectively and command respect as Private Members rather than Party hacks. This is easier if one does not have to meet the demands of a marginal Constituency. Even he was in danger over the E.E.C., and Michael Foot's libertarian support came to his aid as it did to mine.

Whether the topic was divorce, homosexual law reform or abortion, Leo Abse was always deeply involved. By the same token, Roy Jenkins' stewardship at the Home Office saw an unprecedented liberalization of the law and updating of the criminal law. These changes have civilized whole areas of personal life. Unhappily too many so-called militants are so busy demanding complete change in the economic organization of society that they fail to realize that much of the misery suffered by their fellow human beings was precisely within those are as which they studiously avoid or denigrate as liberalism. Perhaps this is the reason why the west European nation which boasts the largest Communist party and a sizeable left-wing Socialist party has given birth to an iconoclastic Radical party. What happened in Italy is reflected in the attitudes of many young people and not a few older ones in

Britain. They see no natural home in the dull and bureaucratic ward meetings of the average Labour Party.

I found it frustrating that the Fridays allocated to Private Members' Bills were often the only days I could get to the Constituency or, for a period, were the days I had to spend at Committee Meetings of the Council of Europe. Private Members' time should not be restricted to a particular day of the week. It should not be allocated and eroded at the whim of the Government. Nor should it be abused by using it to table Bills prepared by the Government but introduced in this time in the certainty of success, whereas more controversial Bills may fail for want of time. Here again, the Executive can largely control the direction of private legislation. Yet it is just when there are no Whips on and a genuine debate and clash of persuasive ideas is taking place that Parliament springs to life and really comes into its own.

Backbenchers may make minor inroads into or additions to Bills at committee stage. Again the Whips select the committees but these standing committees are supposed in theory to be representative of Parliamentary opinion as a whole. A speech on a second reading, when general principles are discussed, often secures a place on the committee which dots and i's and crosses the t's. At least I retain the satisfaction of contributing to the three Race Relations Acts and serving twice on the committee. Similarly I was able play an active Role on the Parliamentary Commissioner Bill which set up the Ombudsman, and had my say on Capital Punishment, The Bail Act, and votes at 18 and Employment Protection Acts. All these fell within the area of law reform which I believe to be the most positive result of Labour periods of office in the last two decades.

There is. a move away from the exclusive allocation of Friday for Members' Bills, but only a handful of the twenty Members drawn out of the hat stand a chance of piloting their Bill into law. Hence the temptation to introduce the short Government drafted Bill and simultaneously achieve the goal of having a Bill passed while receiving the approval of the Party heirarchy.

About 40%, that is eight per session, do get through. Only

a few are significant, but Sir Alan Herbert, Lord Brockway or Sidney Silverman spring to mind as combining luck with ability and persistence. The latter once told me he would give five years of his life to be Home Secretary for a few years. Social issues are always controversial and conservative-minded Home Secretaries can equally be drawn from the Labour Party as recent history shows. Governments have a habit of lagging behind public attitudes on moral and social issues. The one exception was Capital Punishment. Here, as Chairman of the Home Office Group, I was summoned early one morning by Jim Callaghan when he was at the Home Office.

Jim Callaghan could hardly be classed a radical, but he was an astute politician who could gauge the temperature well as he did over Barbara Castle's ill-fated *In Place of Strife*. I had crossed swords with him on the Race Relations Committee and twice beaten him on Amendments by combining with the one Liberal and two enlightened Tories when some of our 'yes-men' were absent. We clashed as a result of his complete lack of understanding of the diminishing role of the Northern Ireland Labour Party and his failure to see the significance of Gerry Fitt's S.D.L.P.

It was with some trepidation that I was ushered into his room. Contrary to all expectations Jim Callaghan was proposing that, instead of waiting for the full five years to elapse as a trial period, we should immediately debate and vote on the issue of Capital Punishment. It was a courageous act. It was also politically astute. It removed the issue a year away from the General Election. Knowing how emotive it could be – my opponent in 1966 had made it his central theme – I readily agreed and offered to muster every support. I can still remember less hardened canvassers coming home in tears in 1966. The Moors murders were fresh in people's memories then, and if there is one issue where logic, statistics, Royal Commissions, and experience abroad all fail to make an impact it seems to be in this area. Curiously, on social issues and Europe, the Labour voter can be more illiberal than the middle-class Conservative.

More down-to-earth, but vital to so many working people in Britain, are the regional debates. The Scottish and

North-Eastern lobby was always well organized, but the North West has been in danger of becoming the Cinderella of England. Its geographical location on the periphery of the E.E.C. after the decline of coal and cotton could turn the cradle of the industrial revolution into its grave. It was for this reason that increasingly I found myself speaking on the economic problems of the area and posing ideas for the expansion of new industry. Combined with adjournment debates such as the 146 airbus project, I knew that Government decisions could mean virtual life or death for British aerospace workers in the Greater Manchester area. This perhaps is the strongest argument against an electoral system based on a national list. Regionalism and concern for regional development ought to be an important feature of an M.P.s work. Our difficulty in the North West was the division between the acute problems of Merseyside (a development area), the former cotton towns of North Lancashire and the concentrated industrial complex of greater Manchester. A cohesive lobby of the kind perfected by Scottish and North-Eastern Members was difficult to create.

One more way of lobbying or at least drawing attention to a problem in the House is the Early Day Motion. This is simply the collection of signatures appended to a motion printed on the Order Paper. It can be used to refer to at Weekly Business Question Time which follows Thursday's Questions. It also allows Members to ask for a debate on matters they regard as priorities. Both these uses permit an expression of the size and strength of a viewpoint. The increasing popularity of Early Day Motions has no doubt devalued their effectiveness. They do remain, however, one method of stating one's position and can be a yardstick of the measure of support for a viewpoint. Very occasionally they may push a Government in a particular direction; on the other hand they may only let off steam and reduce the pressure.

In our current system the Party Meeting is more important in changing policy than any other medium. A concerted onslaught on Eric Varley's plan to increase night fuel prices rocked the Government and forced a concession. One's own supporters have to be placated even if a Government can ride roughshod over the House. I made few speeches at Party Meetings but the most effective was the last, and it pointed me in the direction that led me out of Westminster.

It was directed against the decision of Merlyn Rees to deport the radical American journalist Mark Hosenball. The grounds were never disclosed. Hosenball himself did not know the reason. The Home Secretary seems to have listened to the siren voices of civil servants and security men to whom the tradition of investigatory journalism was anathema. I had worked closely with Mark and others in investigations that were like minor versions of *All the President's Men*. After my speech Ian Mikardo told me there was nothing more to be said; but nothing would move Rees although the meeting unanimously opposed him. The irony is that, with our official secrets procedures and libel laws, a British Nixon could never be removed, a British Watergate could not be exposed and those who tried to do so would be subject to ridicule, legal action, and harassment.

On the other hand George Cunningham and I did suceed in reversing the bipartisan policy on internment without trial in Northern Ireland. Of course we were then in opposition which made it that much easier. Tony Benn was particularly receptive among the leadership. This policy was not only morally wrong, it was the greatest recruiting Sergeant for the I.R.A. The moral may be that party leaders are more receptive and less preoccupied or guarded in opposition. It may be because they have no civil servants to rely on. It could also be, however, that they just do not have the patronage they have in Government.

Being a backbencher may be frustrating but dismissal from the front bench following a rebellion can be almost Orwellian, as one has to acclimatize to being an unperson. Visits abroad, selection for committees and meetings with visiting politicians may suddenly cease. The perks of patronage in the hands of the Whips are denied. In 1970 I was selected to visit the forces in Hong Kong and Singapore, an experience few would turn down, but as I was moving house that week I had to refuse. The following year I asked to go in the light of my previous selection. I did not receive a reply. By then I was one of the seven frontbenchers removed in order to encourage the others. Happily the Inter-Parliamentary Union, Commonwealth Parliamentary Association and various other groups to which I belonged are not controlled by the Whips. Dick Crossman once commented to me that the way to success was to follow the Party line slavishly or to be such a nuisance that you had to be bought off.

Perhaps the most valuable thing I miss as an ex-Member is the opportunity Parliament gives as a sounding board for ideas and campaigns. In founding the Campaign For Democracy in Ulster, or the Manchester-based anti-National Front Organization Democratic Defence, with Eddie Loydon, Neil Kinnock and that well known Liverpool Liberal Trevor Jones 'the vote', the initials M.P. were invaluable. Similarly I was able to spearhead the anti-cult movement in Family Action Information and Rescue (F.A.I.R.). One could sponsor and help organize other pressure groups and play a part in shaping their policy to a greater extent than outsiders. After all one was a professional devoting all one's time to politics.

M.P.s may not be highly regarded but it is to them that all sorts of campaigns and pressure groups turn. They are the focus of protests; of new ideas, and inevitably too of the attentions of cranks. The death threats I received from time to time were a normal part of the M.P's mail! If the waste paper basket is his most useful tool this is not through cynicism. The number of organizations sending circulars and propaganda as against those requiring a reply came to about eighty per cent. Of course many Constituents and others preferred the personal meeting so that figure in isolation could be misleading.

Many members used the Ten-Minute Rule Bill which followed Question Time. Again it allows one to obtain publicity for the need to change on existing law. The Chamber is not empty as in the adjournment debate, and a speech against and a vote may follow. Few get any further, and many bring odium to the Member as the House waits to get on with an important debate. There is the danger of being regarded as a bore unless the topic is of wide interest. Under the Crossman

experiments, which included morning sittings, these were rel-
egated to the end of business. That was an infringement of
the Private Members' rights but I personally consider the
time allocated could be reduced and given to backbenchers
in some other more constructive way. As it is the Ten-Minute
Rule Bill is rather like an indigestible sandwich between
Question Time and the opening speech of a debate.

It is therefore in reaching the outside world, rather than
within the enclosed world of Parliament, that I most valued
the role of communicator. The sheer volume of Parliamentary
business can sap one's energy and enthusiasm even in that
area. Perhaps some of the fault lies in a misunderstanding of
the role of Parliament itself. In *The Commons in the Seventies*,
Walkland and Ryle conclude that the Commons is 'more than
a football stadium where the crowd may cheer and boo!', an
analogy I have frequently chosen myself. 'It is as a critical
forum, not as a governing body that the House of Commons
must be assessed.'

Such criticism can only succeed if Members are armed with
access to information, undeterred by the powers of the Executive, assisted in research and briefed against the battery of
civil servants behind each Minister. These have highly specialized knowledge and tend by instinct and background to
be conservative in the wider sense of the term. That is not to
deny that the critical function of the ordinary Members
backed by public opinion cannot on occasion force Ministers
to rethink and modify their policies. Such occasions are too
rare.

The art of resisting criticism can be elevated into phrases
such as 'the smack of firm Government' or 'refusing to seek
short-term popularity or expediency'. It may be sheer
bloody-minded miscalculation, as occurred over the ill-fated
Suez episode. All too often individual Members or groups are
capable of acquiring more knowledge and expertise than the
conventional wisdom of government departments will con-
cede. When debating the Lancaster Canal I remember with
amusement Eric Heffer walking into the Chamber and com-
menting that it was dangerous to listen to debates – they
tended to make one vote against one's own Government. In

any event, as Bruce Headey commented in a well-researched examination of British Cabinet Ministers, less than one third see themselves as innovators. The rest carry out their duties rather like administrators or public relations officers.

On Standing Committees Members have more chance of altering details of legislation. Even this can be reversed if totally unacceptable to the Minister when the Bill comes back to the House for the Report Stage, at which point the final amendments are made before a Bill goes to the Lords. The Constitutional method of time-tabling a Bill can be right in principle. Like the guillotine which ends debate at a certain time it usually means that many parts of the Bill are not scrutinized at all. The most blatant example was the Industrial Relations Bill.

As the Whips select the Committees – and matters of detail rather than substance are most vulnerable to an adverse vote – the Government of the day normally has an almost unfettered control over legislation, subject only to the caveats outlined. Frequently the main role of Government backbenchers is to shut up in order to hasten business; that of Opposition is to talk at length to little avail. In moving amendments one courts the unpopularity of one's colleagues. The irony is that these suggestions are often written into the next Bill on the same topic five or ten years later.

If this sounds cynical it is because the Parliamentary process makes little provision for the examination of abuses of power. These may not merely be on the part of Government. The blank wall I came up against when investigating powerful bodies such as South African Security or pseudo-religious cults with wide business interests was equally frightening. Similarly there should be more room for scrutiny of giant corporations or Trade Unions. Many official secrets ought to be public property. Congressional Committees in the U.S.A. can call for witnesses, while we are taking only the first tentative steps towards the Committee system. There is too little accountability to that critical forum that the House constitutes.

An experienced M.P. like Richard Hornby mirrored the views of the former father of the House, George Strauss:

The Member's Positive Role

'The record of recent years shows relatively few examples of the backbenches exercising real power and altering the decisions of the Government once they have been taken and publicly announced.'

CHAPTER EIGHT

M.P. in Athens

As an M.P. one may be fortunate enough to go abroad on delegations with the Inter-Parliamentary Union or the Commonwealth Parliamentary Association. These, like directorships, consultancies and other forms of additional payment, may be perfectly legitimate on the one hand, or a form of corruption in the wider sense of the term, on the other. Not a few M.P.s have had a direct interest in espousing the cause of a foreign dictatorship, say Franco's Spain or the Colonels' Greece. Perhaps my most vivid memories concern being asked by Greek Democrats to visit Athens in 1968 and 1969 when I was on the Human Rights Sub-Committee of the Council of Europe. If I had done nothing else in my fifteen years in the House, some of my friends concerned with human rights believe that this would have made my Membership worthwhile. Perhaps I could never forget those words of Byron:

> The mountains look on Marathon
> And Marathon looks on the sea
> And Musing there an hour alone,
> I dream'd that Greece might still be free.

The main phrase that comes to my mind from my study of Greek is 'in the assembly'. It is perhaps significant that the identification of democracy with Greece – the birthplace of Government by the people – made the yoke of the Spartan Colonels so much more difficult to bear. Since a student I had collected clothes and money for Greek political prisoners, and when I was asked to go to Greece on the way back from a Council of Europe meeting in Turkey I was both excited and apprehensive.

At Athens airport, I showed my passport, hoping that my

designation as a Member of Parliament would not arouse suspicion. I had three days in which to see the strong-arm men of the Greek Junta and one of those was a Sunday. My first task, after finding an unobtrusive base, was to contact the British Embassy.

From my room in a cheap but adequate hotel in Plaka, the colourful district clinging to the foot of the Acropolis, I could look out of the window directly upon the Parthenon, bathed in sunlight and appearing unearthly. I was really in the city where democracy had been born. Acting on the advice of my colleague John Fraser, who had been deported from Greece for laying a wreath at the statue of Byron with the stanza above, I phoned a member of the Embassy staff who had been particularly helpful. Within minutes I had arranged an appointment with our Ambassador who had the same name as our Foreign Secretary, Michael Stewart.

I took advantage of the time to make contact with members of the opposition, discreetly using outside telephones, and arranged an evening rendezvous in the suburb of Nea Smyrna. With an hour to spare I set out on foot to the Acropolis, and I have never had such a rewarding climb. Shimmering in the sunlight, the columns stood in timeless symmetry as I gazed over the rooftops of Athens as far as the mountains and the sea. I have yet to discover another such place where I could have stayed interminably, treading the rocks and stones that had seen so much history. It was as if the dialogues of Plato or the philosophy of Aristotle had merged with the satire of Aristophanes to prove that all that Athens had preserved while the enemy was at their gates could not be destroyed by a few bull-necked colonels.

In the spacious atmosphere of the Embassy, I sipped tea and nibbled cake as I became increasingly impressed at our ambassador's grasp of the Greek political scene. Impatient at the apparent timidity of the other Michael Stewart, I had previously taken the view that we should have withdrawn our embassy from Athens. Now I began to have my doubts as the panorama of Greece under the Colonels was sketched out for me.

I explained the reason for my visit; a group of young men

belonging to Rigos Feros had been arrested on the trumped-up charge of planting a bomb in Athens. They had been held incommunicado for sixty days without a change of clothes or a visitor. No lawyer had been allowed to see them. Rumours of torture had filtered out from prison. Visitors to other prisoners had seen blood-stained clothing and had smuggled out messages. The use of the Falanga – the torture of Turkish origin which involves beating the soles of the feet with iron bars – was alleged. The Council of Europe had already obtained tangible evidence of similar practices. There was, at the very least, a prima facie case. I wanted to see the authorities concerned. In particular, I wanted to see the prisoners, more particularly Sotoris Anastasiadis, a young man alleged to be the ringleader of the group. I realized that a Friday afternoon was a bad time to arrive. If necessary I would prolong my stay a day but I had to be back in Parliament the following Tuesday. I was given to understand the Embassy would do what it could.

Naturally, I was less than optimistic about my chances when I met a relative of the accused. That night I was whisked from one room to another; from one taxi to another; in all directions so that I hardly knew where I was. In what appeared to be a printers office I met leaders of the opposition who embraced me like a brother. The gratitude shown by these people that someone from Britain should take an interest in their country was moving in the extreme. They seemed to have an extravagant faith in the influence of a very minor young backbencher. Eventually I arrived at the nerve-centre of the Liberal Opposition. No doubt some of those I had met along the network were Communists. I asked no questions, for in Greece there was little time for quarrels among those opposed to the Junta.

I learned that just prior to my arrival Mr. Kavounides, director of Greek Information Services for thirty years, had been arrested after visiting these very premises. Did the secret police know of their location? The head of the organization was a person of impeccable liberal background. Hard to accept was the almost amateurish precautions taken by them. Unlike the more militant opposition, they were unused to clandestine activities. Conspiracy was not in their line. The picture they painted was depressing. The grip of the Colonels was secure and increasingly repressive. I was given a run-down on the plight of political prisoners and detainees. Many had been deported to small islands. Others were being tortured in notorious prisons and the names of the torturers were handed to me. Late at night, I slipped out unobtrusively into the street; broke into a run at the corner, and wended my way through narrow streets, stopping to listen for footsteps. No one was following. Locating a main road, I orientated myself on the map and returned to the hotel.

To my astonishment, a message was waiting for me. I was to see Mr. Stamatopoulos, the Minister in charge of information (or propaganda) the following day, and Mr. Patakos, a leading colonel in the Junta, had granted me an interview. The Embassy had worked pretty smartly and without its intervention nothing could have been arranged so smoothly. Those who had argued at our Party meeting in favour of keeping diplomatic channels open seemed to be making their point. But Patakos was known for his contempt of democracy. It was he who was known for his visits to Greek farmers informing them that 'I wipe my boots on democracy'. I was resolved that he was going to wipe no boots on me even if I was in no position to wipe the floor with him. A combination of tact, diplomacy, courtesy and stubborn firmness were called for. Greek charm can be persuasive and several Parliamentarians had just reported that everything in the Greek garden was rosy.

I dropped into bed, wishing someone had installed air conditioning or stopped the unpleasant smell of stale soap that came from the bathroom. The numerous images of an exciting day that started at Izmir and finished in the central headquarters of resistance to the Colonels merged with an uneasy sleep. The boots of Mr. Patakos and the bloodstained feet of Sotoris Anastasiadis mingled. Saturday could not come too soon.

As I entered the Ministry building I was ushered along passages and stairs to the office of Mr. Stamatopoulos. Allegedly a former Socialist, his defection and appointment were intended to give some credibility to the idea that Greece's new rulers were representative of various shades of opinion. What was to emerge was that unlike Fascism, which at least has a mass base built on demagogy, Greek military dictatorship depended upon nothing but its own physical power and the inability of any other group to challenge it.

The usual pretexts of preventing a Communist coup; of cleaning up Greek politics; of being a temporary expedient before launching a new democracy were all trotted out dutifully by Stamatopoulos. He knew nothing about political prisoners and could therefore discuss neither them nor their alleged torture. It was apparent that he was no more than Patakos's side kick, a pitiful figure who had sold out to the regime either because of genuine despair at the left or more likely for personal convenience. His words lacked conviction and if I were head of a public relations firm, I would not have given him a job. The call that Patakos was ready to see me came as a relief since blank ignorance of the whereabouts and circumstances of prisoners was all I could elicit from Mr. Stamatopoulos.

Accompanied by an 'interpreter' – English and French had so far served me well enough – I entered the ample office of Patakos. I remember little of the decor – something martial but simple on the wall. There was no doubt that the severe, primitive, close-cropped Patakos had a presence – and even a curious sort of brutal charm as he ushered me in. He was a man of conviction who believed in his mission to cleanse the Greek nation of everything from Communists to miniskirts, even if, by the way, this involved the destruction of democracy, the expulsion of the Monarch, the torture of prisoners and terror in Greek gaols. My interview with him is one of the most memorable experiences I have had, for he was a man of strong will and passion. He strongly resented my presence but either hoped that I would be pliable or that I would be placated by the fact that he had so readily agreed to meet me.

Through the interpreter we came to the point directly; the men were guilty and had to be interrogated. To an English lawyer, the assumption was incredible. Why was no lawyer allowed to see them? – He might pass on messages. How could they prepare a defence? – They were guilty. Then why had they not been brought to trial? – They had to be interrogated. Then you do not know if they are guilty if they have not confessed? – We know they are guilty. Thus we went on. The elementary human right to be charged or released was a strange concept to Patakos.

So far we had talked through his personal interpreter who was far more nervous than I. But when I began to press the question of torture there was an explosion. Patakos could speak quite tolerable English. 'There is no torture in Greece,' he affirmed. 'Talk about anything else, but I refuse to discuss torture.' So we talked about why half the judiciary had been sacked and why there was no move towards an elected Government as had been promised. The replies were unconvincing and gradually I moved the conversation back to torture.

At this juncture I was told that, like the Amnesty International representative who had apparently occupied the same chair as me, I was a Communist Agent. If I burst my sides laughing at this point, Mr. Patakos was certainly taken aback. 'I would be doing the same thing in Poland or Hungary,' I replied; 'I am concerned only about human rights and have just been attending the sub-committee of the Council of Europe on human rights (where the Dutch Social Democratic M.P. Mr. Van der Stoel had been giving a magnificent lead on the Greek question).'

Altogether, we spent over one hour and a half locked in oral combat. As I left I noticed a queue of twenty or so people, including high ranking clergymen of the Greek Orthodox Church, waiting for an audience. They looked at me oddly and grumbled audibly. I felt rather good about that until I noticed that the 'interpreter' insisted on accompanying me to the hotel. 'Damn it,' I thought, politely trying to refuse the courtesy offered, 'now they will know my whereabouts and place someone on my tail.'

I went up onto the roof for lunch. As I looked out over Athens with its churches, narrow streets, and large boulevards leading from omonia to Constitution Square, the contrast between this beautiful sunny scene dominated by the Acropolis behind me and the squalid regime which presided over it struck me forcibly. I had hardly eaten since my arrival and began to tuck into my moussaka. The phone rang and I was wanted. Would I phone Mr. Patakos in ten minutes? – a direct line to the strongest man in Greece. Even after rubbing shoulders with Prime Ministers, top diplomats and army brass from all over Europe, this special treatment still seemed strange. Surely he had not changed his mind and was allowing me to see the prisoners in order to prove his denial of inhumane treatment and torture?

Ten minutes later I was speaking to Patakos; no Secretary announced me on the line. It was obviously a private line to the man himself. He was curiously friendly 'How would you like a good time?' he asked. 'I didn't come to Greece for a good time,' I replied, 'I came to see the prisoners and you will not allow me to visit them.' 'Never mind that, I'm flying to the Peloponese at six this evening. You will be my special guest. You'll have a good time. The tickets can be ready immediately and you can stay as long as you want. I assure you that you will have a good time.' The kind of 'good time' left little room for doubt, but feeling almost as if I were reciting righteous lines from some morality play I countered, 'I would be severely compromised if I accompanied you as your guest and went home without seeing the prisoners.'

It occurred to me that he might want to compromise me. Alternatively, introductions in Greek as 'my good friend the Labour M.P.', and photographs along with him would make good propaganda in the Greek press. My five gullible colleagues on the recent all-party delegation had certainly fallen for the usual treatment meted out on tours – guided of course – in totalitarian states where they have no knowledge of the language or contacts in the underground. However, I made one last throw of the dice. 'Of course, if I were allowed to see the prisoners the position might be different.' I admit that turning down a visit to the Peloponese went against my desire to see the world, and we all have our weakness, if it is only the wanderlust. In any event my suggestion was ignored. 'Phone me before four if you change your mind.'

Had I done the right thing? Might I have been able to use

the chance to persuade Patakos to allow me to see the prisoners? I felt my instinct was right, but I was not one hundred per cent sure. I did not want to compromise anyone and I knew that I was now likely to be followed. I quickly changed into typical tourist garb, slung a camera over my shoulder, waited until a taxi passed the front of the hotel and jumped into it, driving to the busiest part of the City. There I got out, doubled back into another taxi coming the other way and dropped off about half a mile from the headquarters of the Resistance. Again I ensured as far as humanly possible that there was no one following before heading for my destination. The street was deserted and I entered another door and waited five minutes. An old lady with her shopping walked past, and there was no sign of anyone in the vicinity when I dodged into the doorway and took the lift to my floor, where I knocked on the door. After an interval it opened slightly and there was an audible sigh of relief. I was almost pulled in. They thought I was the secret police.

To my astonishment, there inside was one of my colleagues who had been in Turkey with me. He had also gone to investigate allegations of torture and to take statements. I met two boys who had been picked up, given the Falanga and still showed the marks: toe nails missing and badly bruised feet. They alleged that they had been strapped to a bunk and beaten with iron bars on the souls of their feet while their shoes were on. They were then left with the shoes on. The most painful part was when their feet swelled within their shoes. Their stories were consistent as I questioned them separately just as I would cross-examine witnesses in court. They had been released with no charge. It was just another example of cat and mouse tactics to demoralize the opposition.

I was strongly advised not to go with Patakos. My instinct had been right. When it was all clear, I left alone, though a little heavier than when I arrived. I will never know what the message was that I carried home to England. On my next visit to Greece I was to learn that Sotoris Anastasiadis and his friends were acquitted of planting the bomb. They were sentenced for belonging to an illegal organization and Anastasiadis was given a sixteen-year sentence. On the day I saw Patakos he and his colleagues were allowed their first change of clothes in sixty days. On the day following my broadcast on the B.B.C. Greek service they ceased torturing him. His mother, an older and sicker person than when I had first met her, could not thank me enough.

It was little enough for me to do and entailed no risk as a British M.P. It was part of my reason for being in the House. I often wonder whether I could face the hardships that exist in totalitarian countries for those who care to speak out. I do not think I would be strong enough to do the same. The least I could do was to use the privilege of living in a democracy in which I enjoyed the status of an M.P. to help Greek democrats, and *they* thanked me. It should have been the other way round.

It was nearly two years later to the day that I again left for Athens. But on this first occasion I had had my 'good time' for, in order to get away from Athens for a day before catching my plane, I had sailed to Aegina Poros and Hydra and savoured the beauty of three of 'The Isles of Greece'. My last view was a sunset over Paereus.

On several occasions subsequently, Greek friends asked me to return but I was overworked and had to face a General Election in my marginal seat. With the election just over and still elated by victory, if physically tired, I agreed at a day's notice to fly out to Athens to observe a trial of opposition groups. This time I was nervous, for neither my entry into Greece or into the trial were assured. Max Van der Stoel had been barred when he went on behalf of the Council of Europe. Ray Dobson M.P. had failed to gain entry to a trial – and he a policeman's son. John Fraser M.P. had been deported. I was frankly worried as I went through passport control, and it was with relief that I boarded the bus and talked with a casual stranger from the United States. We were next to meet in the courtroom. He was there for the same purpose as I.

Although I encountered no difficulty in entering the country, I did not contact a defence counsel until 12.20 a.m. on Monday, since he was not at home when first called. We arranged to meet outside the court at 8 a.m. I arrived at the court building at 7.55 a.m. There were several police and some soldiers in the vicinity, together with special lorries for transporting military personnel.

I asked to be allowed in, but was continually blocked by police (armed, but with arms in holsters). I stood my ground, but a policeman pushed me away, claiming that the defence lawyer would not arrive until 9 a.m. When he did arrive, after some conversation, cajoling, and charming this lawyer helped me through the police cordon to the admission office. At first, entry was refused, as I had no permit, but after a brief explanation I was allowed into the trial on depositing my passport. I was then frisked by the police, and my case was examined before I was allowed past. This procedure became routine but more formal and less hostile – indeed almost apologetic – until on my final visit they did not even bother to frisk me. There appeared to be a softening of attitudes towards the foreign observers as the trial proceeded, and at 10 p.m. on the first day we were formally presented to the President of the Tribunal who was very correct towards us while I was present.

As the prisoners assembled I counted seventeen armed police and soldiers in the court room, which in its simplicity resembled some minor magistrate's court in Britain. Six high-ranking military officers in smart uniforms took their places and the Military Tribunal – or Court Martial – was in session. Before them were a number of large dossiers which remained unopened, only the clerk, another officer, taking notes and reading the indictment, sitting on the left of the Tribunal. The Prosecutor, whose role appeared subordinate to that of the police chief, Mallias, who was to dominate the proceedings, sat on the right of the Tribunal and opened the case against the accused very briefly before calling the chief witness for the Prosecution, Superintendent Mallias at approximately 9 a.m.

In the dock were the eleven accused, showing remarkably little sign of strain. The chief accused, Kaloudis – with whose Communist views I naturally have not the slightest sympathy as an old style Communist – impressed me in particular with his calm and inner strength of will. He told me that there had been no physical torture, although prison conditions were not good. He spoke of psychological torture, but had no time to elaborate as Police Sergeant 12398 caused me to break off our conversation. Of the three women in the dock, one held a battery-operated fan, and another young woman smiled fondly at her husband who was among the few members of the public present at the trial. A dark young woman with classical features smiled stoically in spite of the ten-year sentence possibly awaiting her. All were dressed in civilian clothes and showed no signs of ill-treatment. Their families were allowed to take them refreshments. About thirty people were in court, some of them security men in plain clothes.

Opportunity to speak to prisoners or lawyers came at about two or three hourly intervals during the day. The trial lasted on Monday from 8:30 a.m. to 2 p.m. and 6 p.m. to 1:10 a.m. (twelve hours, forty minutes) something quite unheard of in my own experience, but evidently intended to finish in one day – although it was to continue for part of Tuesday from 8:30 a.m. The physical and mental strain on those involved was something quite unknown in normal legal circles – even in courts martial. The prisoners expressed gratitude for our presence.

In the spartan courtroom the first legal objection came as Superintendent Mallias was about to be called.

Apparently a statement had recently been made that after a certain date there would be an end to military tribunals and a reversion to civil processes of law.

The Defence lawyers submitted that they had received the dossiers on the accused 6 days before the trial. Their only opportunity to speak to the accused was on three occasions for two hours each time, during a period of visits from families and in the presence of the police. They demanded time to prepare their defence for trial before a civil court. This submission was dismissed. A curious feature of the trial lay in the fact that the defendants were seated together on one side of the courtroom guarded by police. The lawyers were on the other side, and no communication passed between them. There was therefore no method by which defendants could instruct their advocates. The advocates wanted a month to prepare their defence. In a trial of this nature the request was by no means unreasonable.

Moreover, the charge of attempting to overthrow the social order by force was of such a serious nature and the dossiers (which incidentally remained unopened on the Tribunal's desk) so large, that an adjournment should have been permitted for the preparation of the defence, if the defence was to have any meaning.

Superintendent Mallias took the oath before the President of the Tribunal. He first gave evidence with virtually no prompting by the Prosecuting Officer – rather like a policeman in a minor magistrate's court in England. He produced two copies of *Rizospastis*, the clandestine newspaper, and outlined the history of the Greek Communist Party, Russian Communism and Communism in general. He read a good deal from notes. Standing in the centre of the court before the President, he continued with this general critique of Communist ideology. The defendants listened with interest, raising a hand from time to time, and Kaloudis attempted to intervene. The President then asked questions from what appeared to be depositions. The Police Superintendent adopted the manner of a politician rather than a witness, speaking eloquently with expansive gestures, and a ready answer when interrogated. His role was clearly political rather than that of a factual police witness.

Among foreign press circles, he is alleged to have been the chief interrogator responsible for torture but this was merely the view of press representatives of various nationalities.

Kaloudis stood up but was told to sit down by the President, and the long harangue by Mallias continued. At one point he told a defendant to sit down, not waiting for the President.

Following this testimony a lawyer posed questions and spoke freely, and several heated exchanges took place. It was rather as if in the absence of a Parliament, the courtroom was the only place for the expression of political dissent and for open debate. Ideas, not facts, were on trial. There was an absence of any formal procedure. The atmosphere was one of political confrontation. The accused themselves followed a similar but shorter routine of challenging the police witnesses.

Their case, as put to me by the accused personally, was that they did not intend to overthrow the regime by force, but that force would become the only option if the government continued on its present path. This was consistent with their general political line.

A particularly interesting debate took place between lawyer Mangakis and Superintendent Mallias.

A second police witness added nothing new and the same but shorter procedure was followed. Again there was no direct proof of connection between articles written and individual defendants. One of the Tribunal then read a long list of articles allegedly found on the accused when arrested.

Defence witnesses were called, apparently as to character, but they were inaudible. (A young lady, an elderly lady, and a young man.) No exhibits were produced by them, and the only exhibit in the trial appeared to be the copies of *Rizospastis*.

I was shocked at the length of the trial in two ways: (a) a thorough trial would have taken three to four months; (b) there was an unconscionable hurry to finish the trial, which meant sitting from 8 a.m. to 1.10 a.m.

I was also surprised that defendants had the right to cross-examine, in addition to Counsel. It could not be said that there was any attempt to stifle debate, other than the refusal of Mallias to remain silent when contradicted. Again this emphasized his curious role as a witness cum prosecutor.

Kaloudis spoke in his own defence quietly, and in a restrained and dignified manner, for a full hour, followed by other defendants, and then by the lawyers for the defendants. By Greek standards the court was obviously 'free', in the sense that no one was silenced. What offended the liberal conscience was the fact that a group of eleven persons were sentenced to terms of from four years to twenty years, and three to life imprisonment, because they were an organized opposition force in a country without democratic institutions – without any evidence of acts of violence, or of attempted acts of violence.

I understand that after I left the trial, a defence lawyer was sentenced to one year's imprisonment for contempt of court. Many of the defence lawyers had previously served terms of detention on similar charges. This is an indication of the perilous conditions under which members of the legal profession have to work. For a lawyer to do his duty fully on behalf of his client in Greece requires unusual courage and involves him in personal danger.

When I returned to London I was shocked to discover that an account of the trial contained in a paragraph in *The Times* headed 'M.P. Criticises Greek Trial', had been so twisted by the Government Newspaper as to give the impression that I had considered its conduct to be correct. The word 'correct' had been taken out of context. It took a letter to *The Times* to expose this particular expression of Junta contempt for the truth, but unfortunately few Greeks read *The Times*.

During the hectic days and nights of the trial I snatched a little sleep in a room that was more like a sauna bath. My return to a Spartan courtroom had been less dramatic than my introduction to Athens. But the Acropolis still stood in timeless witness to the birth of democracy. Meanwhile students were being goaled in England because they acted violently in protest at an evening's entertainment given in order to enhance the image of Greece abroad.

Though their actions may not be defended the thoughts that prompted them must have come from the same pages of Aristotle's ethics that I myself read as a student of law. Perhaps those who passed sentence had ceased to remember them. Perhaps they had ceased to muse or dream as they sat daily meting out justice which the Athenians had considered central to man's dealings with man in the 'plis'. But there were still some of us who shared with Byron the dream 'That Greece might still be free.'

If the visit to Athens stands out it is because the achievement of preventing another human being from being tortured must in retrospect have made being an M.P. worthwhile. I also enjoyed the novelty and excitement. So long as one builds a barrier against possible corruption, the contact with foreign diplomats and politicians and the opportunities to see and understand the world are an undoubted attraction of an M.P.'s demanding life.

As a young M.P. I was offered a crate of wine by a Rumanian diplomat for Christmas. He could not understand my refusal of the wine and yet my willingness to accept the gift of a novel. He also wanted to know if there were any Social Democrats in exile at an International Union of Socialist Youth Conference which I had addressed in Luxemburg. When he persisted in asking – after I told him there were not but if there were I would not tell him – I severed diplomatic relations. By contrast I had no qualms at accepting a fee of £15 for an article in the Czech writer's magazine. This was then leading the struggle for Socialism with a human face which ended with the Warsaw Pact countries snuffing out the embers of democracy and, incidentally, ensuring that my second article and the magazine itself were never to appear.

Members have to make their own minds up about what they regard as ethical. Certainly I was never paid a penny for numerous lectures in France where my knowledge of the language and ability to deal with Mayors, préfets and journalists were made use of by the Government. It was hard work but an education in itself.

After a visit to the Leipzig Trade Fair organized by the East West Trade Group, which I came to mistrust, Norman Buchan and I were invited explicitly to use our positions as M.P.s to tour Eastern Europe selling on behalf of a Company. My copy of the letter went into the waste paper bin. Norman was so incensed that he took his to Willy Ross. However, not a few M.P.s seem to be able to use the House as a pivot from which fortunes in business and consultancies are made. That is why I could never understand the hostility to genuine professional men who derived their qualifications from the period before they entered the House. There was a particular hostility to barristers, which was only justified where the barrister regarded the House as a sideline or club. An outside alternative does give an M.P. more room for freedom from pressures.

Though the Whips have tremendous powers of patronage

in sending people abroad, one takes one's turn for the I.P.U. and C.P.A. delegations with which I went to Mauritius, Ethiopia and the Caribbean. All my other visits came because of a special interest in an area or because of my two-year membership of the Council of Europe. That appointment arose from a throw-away line to an influential member of the delegation who had noted my growing interest in the European scene.

Membership was not all fun and games although the human rights Sub-Committee had four days in Turkey which was pathetically striving to show its Europeanism. Most European democracies were represented, even Malta had a deputation among whom I made some close friends. My maiden speech on the Committee was on the expulsion of Greece, and my last contribution on the treatment of minorities in non-member countries ranging from Spain to the U.S.S.R. The usual routine for legal and political committee meetings was a late flight to Paris on Thursday night and a return to the Constituency for the Saturday Advice Bureau. Usually all I saw of Paris was from the airline bus. There was an interval at Rome and Salzburg and three weeks per year in full session at Strasbourg. There I was rapporteur on measures to be taken to outlaw discrimination on the grounds of race, religion, nationality or sex. In this I followed Ivor Richard who was to become our Ambassador to the United Nations after losing his seat in Parliament.

The topics followed my own Home Office interest on entering the House and included the position of migrant workers in Europe. Basically, these were human rights topics, and even if we could not legislate, we could act as a catalyst. The Council had no legislative powers. It was organized along Party and not National lines in a hemicycle with a strong committee system. One made prepared speeches and rarely had to think on one's feet. The secretariat did the hard slog on most reports. It was the antithesis, therefore, of the Westminster system, with no cut and thrust. It may have been a talking shop but it carried some weight, and national Parliaments sometimes took note of its recommendations. Bill Rodgers was leader of the British delegation which was on average about half the age of its veteran European counterparts. Geoffrey Rhodes, Alan Lee Williams, Maurice Miller, Shirley Summerskill, Sam Silkin, Bob Maclennon and others like them were gaining valuable experience rather than being put out to graze. Maurice Edelman, who typified the accomplished backbencher who was amazingly never to become a Minister, was by comparison a senior member. By and large, it was a talented and vigorous group rather than a pay-off for past services. This may be because of the nature of the 1964 and 1966 intakes into the House. It may also be because Bill Rodgers, as a junior Minister in the Foreign Office dedicated to the European ideal, took it seriously.

There was a lighter side to the innocent M.P. abroad which I described in an article for *The Blackley Guardian*, in spite of my agent's misgivings. Had she heard of some of my exploits in sabotaging a mafia man's car in the Caribbean, being shot at in Sinai or breaking protocol by using my legs instead of a cadillac and disappearing into the immense market of Addis Abbaba she might have disapproved more strongly. In fact my Constituents enjoyed it. Perhaps they liked the idea of an M.P. with a feeling for adventure. If one only goes where one's hosts want one to go one will only see what they want one to see. That is not the way to learn the truth. Too many Members succumb to this through flattery or naïveté. By venturing into the world behind the scenes I could form the sort of judgement which might have permitted us to see the futility of Suez; see the very real fears of the Israelis overlooked by the Golan heights, forsee the coming revolution in an impoverished and divided Ethiopia or the political tensions in a Caribbean dominated by greed and Geest as it flexed its newly independent muscles. It is a lesson I had learned as a student when we were still propping up the unpopular Iraqi regime. Anyone who had bothered to get to know what Iraqi friends told me would have forseen Nuri es Said's demise, if not his being torn to pieces in the streets of Bagdhad. Born into certain circles and moving in even more restricted ones, too many of our diplomats have blinkers imposed by their public school and Oxbridge backgrounds. A few more drawn from the red brick universities or the factories of the world

most of us inhabit might recognize the realities and find
common ground with the ordinary people who, in the last
analysis, make history.

CHAPTER NINE

The Changing Face
of Westminster

My horizons were significantly widened, and my method of examining foreign news perceptibly modified as a result of my experiences abroad. M.P.s should be given a modest travel allowance to take them once each year, during the recess or, if necessary, during a crisis, to some sphere in which they have a special interest. This may happen now when a Committee has to examine matters abroad. And it is in the sphere of the Committee system, linked to departmental responsibility, that we are beginning to see one of the biggest changes in the face of Westminster.

The committee system is still in a formative stage and its success will depend upon its powers and the way it is used. There does seem to be a general recognition now that long-standing procedures at Westminster, and even the electoral system itself, should be looked at more critically. This is essential, for if institutions do not adapt to current needs then the result can be catastrophic. Our basic conservatism is keeping us at the foot of the European League Table. The twilight of empire still preserved Parliament as a gentleman's club but the proposal for a seven storey office block containing 400 offices and a swimming pool to replace the inadequate accommodation, in which as many as fourteen Members share an office, would take five years to complete, and that assumes that it is ever started.

There were experiments in Dick Crossman's day. Morning sittings proved unhelpful, however, when Parliament continued to sit half the night as well. On the other hand the family room still exists and, most serious of all, the experimental select committees dealing with specific topics have now been broadened so that all aspects of Government activity can be scrutinized more closely. The desire for change was illustrated in a debate on procedure held on the 2 February 1976. By June of that year a Select Committee had been set up to consider the practice and procedure of the House of Commons and to make recommendations for the more effective performance of its functions.

Its first report was published on the 17 July 1977 after sixty-eight meetings. Significantly, sub-committees were set up to look at the Committee system in Canada, to examine the method of dealing with statutory instruments and E.E.C. documents. These may be particularly important but Members have little chance in practice to influence their contents. Indeed the method of delegating powers to Ministers in Acts of Parliament is a twentieth-century scourge as society becomes more complex. A member is fortunate if he manages a comment on the few that are debated, usually between ten o'clock and half past eleven at night but often later. Indeed there is insufficient scrutiny of the ever-increasing volume of delegated legislation. In addition, the problem has been aggravated by the need to scrutinize E.E.C. legislation or directives. It would be unthinkable to off-load all this directly on to the floor of the House, but a committee system can filter it. Similarly the Reports of Committees should be debated on the floor of the House and their recommendations embodied in motions and voted on. It should not be left to the Whips to decide business but a business committee could better recognize the wishes and needs of the House. Opposition and Private Members' time, together with a reasonable time for legislative measures by Government, suitably time-tabled for adequate debate, must be safeguarded. This would be an improvement on the present haphazard and wasteful system.

The very idea of committees sitting simultaneously with the Chamber was a Crossman innovation which has survived; but when Members start sitting through the night on Committee, as they did on the Steel Bill, one sees the tendency again for debate to expand in order to fill the time available for its completion, however long. My own impression is that this growing complexity was eroding the already limited powers of backbenchers. This is particularly so in monitoring the actions of Government departments and setting the limits on Executive power.

The urgent need is for control by Parliament of the Executive. If this is done by a powerful Committee system, linked to ministries, it would elevate the powers of the whole of Parliament, contrary to the arguments of detractors of the Committee system, such as that most brilliant of debaters, Michael Foot. Today there is not only frustration but a trivialization of issues. Unfetterred discretion is too often placed in the hands of Ministers. In reality that usually means a cabinet committee whose workings are secret, or the unseen hand of the civil service. Accountability to the elected representative of Blackley or anywhere else is largely a myth in a self-perpetuating establishment. As I write, the development of the Committee system – opposition to secrecy spearheaded by radical reporters and a growing number of M.P.s – may make Mark Hosenball and Duncan Campbell martyrs to the system defended by Merlyn Rees as Labour Home Secretary and an outmoded official Secrets Act.

Even more curiously, in the light of the developing Committee system, another former M.P., Brian Sedgemore, who was himself a civil servant before spending five years in the House – two of them as P.P.S. to Anthony Wedgwood Benn – has been studying the scene through the eyes of a Member involved in the Department of Energy.* He does not suggest remedies but his identification of the centres of power is far removed from those given in conventional constitutional text books.

He names the Prime Ministerial nature of our Government as the first centre of power. A Prime Minister can dissolve a Government; make or break Ministers or P.P.S.s as happened to us both for different reasons. Most of his decisions are secret and he enjoys remarkable powers of patronage. Secondly Sedgemore names the centralized nature of public and

* *The Secret Constitution*

private institutions. Indeed the state may own the mines, the railways or the steel industry but every M.P. knows the severe limit set on what may or may not be asked about them. Thirdly he refers to the development in the civil service in Britain and the E.E.C. of a political power and authority that lies outside the concept of Ministerial responsibility.

Clearly private institutions are not answerable to Parliament, but there are some limits. The secret services and the military establishment are not mentioned. Sedgemore does add, however, two slightly nebulous concepts – the acceptance by all modern Governments of the conventional establishment wisdom, and the corporatist nature of Government. He terms this the 'Secret Constitution', the title of his book. In spite of our political differences and priorities, his conclusions, illustrated in depth by the Department of Energy and buttressed by his emphasis on the Official Secrets Act, are in line with my own. Our main difference lies in the more optimistic belief I have in the ability of radicals in the media, the House, the establishment itself and of plain ordinary people to force even the most secretive and conventional of governments to change direction once in a while. So long as journalists like Duncan Campbell are willing to risk prosecution, and M.P.s are willing to risk promising careers by taking on the establishment, there is hope. But there is something wrong with a form of Government that makes such sacrifices necessary.

That is why the Committee system has great potential and I do not see why Michael Foot fears devaluation of the Chamber and of the standard of debate. The Chamber is seldom overcrowded even though it cannot hold all the Members. Churchill wanted it preserved in its old form after the blitz and one enters through the Churchill arch which has never been repaired. It is packed at the opening and closing of various debates, and usually for such occasions as the Budget and Prime Minister's Question Time, but the Chamber really comes into its own when the Whips are not on, the result of the division uncertain, and when Members actually consider the arguments put forward before voting.

In addition to the emphasis on the Chamber, Members still have to cope with a threefold increase in delegated legislation in thirty years. Questions doubled between the 1940s and the 1970s, as did time spent on Standing Committees. Thus we got the worst of all worlds, without a truly comprehensive committee system and with a Chamber which is rarely central to the Members' activities whatever the myths of the past. Indeed the oratory of a Lloyd George, a Nye Bevan or a Winston Churchill seems to be a thing of the past. The future lies in a different approach, so it seems all the more futile to indulge in the masochistic procedure of the ritual vote. I used to hate tramping through those division lobbies wasting a quarter of an hour each time, when I knew the result was a foregone conclusion; and the division bell rang in the middle of meeting or when one was engaged on some other important matter.

On the Industrial Relations Bill there were in the region of four hundred divisions, a loss of one hundred hours of potential debating time. When we voted through the night non-stop and took time off in turns, that was a gesture of defiance which was hardly appreciated at British Leyland or on Clydeside. Time taken to walk through a lobby, give one's name to a clerk, nod to a teller and resume one's seat or go back whence one came is another unnecessary piece of ancestor worship. To this date no one has devised a better way but no one has really tried.

Even after fifteen years I could and did get lost in those corridors of alleged power. Westminster would make a magnificent museum, but a modern purpose-built Parliament, with offices that allow Members to be near library research facilities and their own secretaries – who may currently be housed five minutes away – should replace the present palace.

One curious by-product of simultaneous sittings of Chamber and Standing Committees is that the latter have to be suspended during a division. The layout of the committee rooms on the first floor is also based on the adversary character of debate, but this is surely highly inappropriate to the new select committees. It is also unhelpful if the committee stage is intended to allow closer backbench scrutiny of legislation, when alliances of a temporary nature are formed which may blur Party divisions. But even here the whipping system is in evidence although less effective than on the floor of the House, where the Committee stage of Bills of major constitutional importance is debated.

There are important objections to Select Committees taking over the work of Standing Committees on Bills. One is that they would revert to becoming battle grounds between the parties rather than diverse backbenchers seeking the truth. The answer is to equip Standing Committees with research facilities and permit them to call for evidence and documents so that they can examine Bills in an informed manner, and already there are signs that the committees are winning the battle for research back-up. Ministries, in the shape of their civil servants, should also be available to submit themselves to cross-examination, perhaps to a more limited extent than before Select Committees because of the time factor.

The Select Committee on procedure sensibly recommended that non-partisan and technical Bills of an urgent nature could go before Select Committees while some Select Committee members should sit on Standing Committees to scrutinize the legislation of their particular departmental interest, and it agreed with my other proposition in suggesting three days for taking evidence from the public on Bills. The merit of all this is the expertise which backbenchers can build up on the work of particular departments. The other is the guidance from or exposure to outside interests, including the civil service, which is a key issue if we are to dismantle that secret constitution.

There must be an absolute right to summon witnesses in positions of power if those concentrations of corporate power are not to replace democratic accountability. Without this power to question Ministers and civil servants and to demand the production of documents M.P.s will remain emasculated. The Committe system would then be in a sense counterproductive. It would give a spurious authenticity to the working of Parliament. It would give the impression of scrutiny without the reality of power. These powers are more important than the form or the name of the committees.

By the same token there is a need to receive evidence from interested parties. The weakness of much legislation today is

that outside interests are consulted when M.P.s themselves
are not. If M.P.s feel that the C.B.I. and T.U.C. have made
their views known to the Minister, while they are not aware
of their views, this heightens their feeling of irrelevance. They
feel that they are facing a *fait accompli*. The feeling that M.P.s
are the last to be consulted and cannot themselves question
the interested parties as a committee is demoralizing to them
and leads to a sort of resigned cynicism.

The Report of the Select Committee on Procedure has been
available since July 1978. Suffice it to say that it was a useful
and important milestone. Many of its recommendations are
worthy of detailed consideration. Some require rapid application or, where already acted on, need strengthening. But
the Committee, in a natural and laudable desire to curb the
powers of the Executive, came out against the time-tabling of
Bills. They pointed out that the Government can already use
the guillotine to curb debate. I would prefer the former to the
latter.

One effect of the guillotine is to stifle debate on large parts
of controversial Bills. What is needed is a fair and flexible
allocation of time to allow all parts of a Bill to be debated
reasonably. I do not regard the right to filibuster as sacrosanct. It is an ineffective and negative approach to elevating
the powers of the ordinary backbencher. In the long run it
achieves nothing. It provokes and justifies the use of the
guillotine so as to become counter-productive. However it is
difficult to forsee which clauses in a Bill may provoke the
most debate.

The House or the Select Committee on Procedure should
be asked to consider a refinement of existing procedures for
time-tabling or another alternative to the guillotine. Clearly
the Select Committee could not initially find a practical sol-
ution within the context of the existing system. However, just
as one now suspends the ten-o'clock rule to allow debate after
ten, a similar procedure might be used to prolong debate on
intricate, important or controversial clauses after an initial
allocation of time. There ought to be a guarantee of debate
on all aspects of a Bill, and nothing can be more unsatisfactory
than falling back on the existing guillotine motion. For that

in itself wastes time as one hears the ritual arguments deployed with cynicism by Governments which opposed them in opposition and Oppositions which proposed them in Government.

One irritating feature of the life of a government backbencher is that, not only is his main function to keep quiet but he can be forced to stay night after night by small groups of Opposition members taking turns. The reason for this is the need to keep a hundred members present for a closure. All these archaic procedures would be so much less sacrosanct in the context of an effective committee system. The Select Committee's suggestion for dealing with Statutory Instruments commends itself. The Departmentally related committees would be free to consider all Statutory Instruments falling within their field of interest. They would be provided with regular information about such Instruments. Prior to this they would of course be considered by the Standing Committee on Statutory Instruments with the added safeguard that this would have added a number of Members from the Departmental Standing Committee, no doubt because of their specialized knowledge. While such changes will undoubtedly add to the burden of committee work and may not appear glamorous, there could be compensation in civilized hours in the Chamber and real control over the Executive.

Similarly the Department Select Committees would perform a similar function in relation to E.E.C. legislation. This would be additional to the Select Committee on European legislation while E.E.C. orders would be filtered through all three nets.

The key recommendations were nos. 31 and 32:

(31) 'There should be a reorganization of the Select Committee Procedure Structure to provide the House with the means of scrutinizing the activities of the public service on a continuing and systematic basis.'

(32) 'The Select Committees should in future be based primarily on the subject areas within the responsibility of individual Government Departments or groups of departments.'

This is now coming to fruition although it is curious that

the Parties themselves have long had such subject groups. I myself was Chairman of the Home Office Group before and the Employment Group after my spell on the Front Bench. What was acceptable for the Parties is now being accepted by the House. Greater opportunity to debate Select Committee Reports was recommended but it fell short of elevating these to debates on motions with votes.

It is when we come to recommendation no. 64 that we come to the crunch: Select Committees should be empowered to order the attendance of Ministers to give evidence to them and order the production of papers and records by Ministers. When this happens Parliament will have made the major breakthrough. It will have broadened the scope of such powers and not allow itself to be fobbed off by the Official Secrets Act. It is the direction in which I hope the newly constituted committees will head.

The suggestion of twelve committees need not be rigidly adhered to although I can see the danger of a proliferation of committees. If each committee only has ten members it will not fulfill the need to have a Parliament where M.P.s can attain a high degree of expertise in, say, three fields of interest. Far from devaluing the House it could add a new dimension of expertise, and even non-Members would have access to the committee reports before they were debated. Devaluation comes about now by reason of a large membership by Jacks-of-all-trades unable to penetrate the armour of Government Departments or obtain specialized information which the Department chooses to withold. It is possible that committees will ultimately become significant initiators of legislation.

Writing in *The Guardian* on 10 December 1979, Kenneth Baker M.P., a Conservative, refers to a 'remarkable decade of change at Westminster'. He makes a number of forecasts, some of which are contained in my own analysis. He claims that the changes now underway were more likely under a Conservative than a Labour Government, although the record of innovation in procedure does neither Party more credit than the other or indeed any credit at all.

The current establishment has a life almost independent of the elector and his representative. The self-perpetuating oligarchy of top civil servants, heads of giant public and private corporations, trades unions and employers' organizations, backed up by an almost presidential system of power and patronage, exists as much under Mrs Thatcher as it did under her predecessors. It fuses with the legal profession through the Lord Chancellor and the Law Officers. Every barrister knows that there are establishment chambers and judges who are largely drawn from these and from a narrow social background. No doubt the same applies to other professions and spills over into the media.

Thus, although avowedly anti-establishment, the Labour and Trade Union Movement have themselves become a powerful establishment. The Peers created by Harold Wilson from among Labour M.P.s and Trade Union Leaders testify to this. The system sucks one in. One plays the game according to the rules with the option either of being bought off or living a lonely maverick existence on the fringes. A new role for M.P.s akin to the investigating journalist will revolutionize the function of Parliament. New mechanisms may be used to block this new power of scrutiny, but it will, if it comes about, be a major factor in changing the face of Westminster.

One dominating feature of the connection between the political and legal establishments is the fact that the Law Officers are part of the Government of the day. The Lord Chancellor sits in the legislature, albeit the House of Lords, and is part of the Executive in the Cabinet. The Attorney General makes political decisions in respect of prosecutions. It is a far cry from Montesquieu's separation of powers. It gives more power and patronage to Government and potential Government. It provides an interlocking matrix of power in an area where I believe there should be strict separation, and an independent prosecuting authority should make decisions without pressures from Parliament, law officers, and Government or police. A Ministry of Justice could then be seized of legal affairs and the idiocy of, for example, the 'A.B.C.' trial on Official Secrets or many metropolitan police prosecutions could be avoided.

That the plague of secrecy is being fought by new allies inside and outside the House is shown by the more recent

Economist Intelligence Unit Report of a study of the Commonwealth Parliamentary Association. This is confined to scrutiny of finance and looks beyond our shores to Commonwealth legislatures. However, finance is the core of many Government Departments. The findings slot in with the idea of departmentally related Select Committees. They can provide the opportunity for close scrutiny of estimates, before they are considered on the floor of the House, as well as general enquiries into the continuing activities of Departments. Public Corporations and the Crown Agents should be answerable to the Public Accounts Committee.

Answerability is becoming the order of the day. Its weakness is that it relies on informal rules and publicity to expose scandals while stressing the need for timely presentation of information. There is a vagueness about how far compulsion is to be permitted in scrutinizing the use of public funds. Nothing is said about private ones. Corporate power is corporate whether private or public. A worker at Ford's, British Leyland or Moscow Dynamo will know that. If the changing face of Westminster is to mean anything it must be to change the face of corporate power. At least we are now seeing the first steps inside the House and some new institutions outside. Meanwhile Parliament itself could grasp a bold initiative with a Freedom of Information Act.

For Parliament to be one step ahead in changing its ways would be to restore public faith in an institution which has been losing public confidence as a truly democratic institution. Such a change of face, combined with the departmental Select Committees endowed with real powers, would make that face hardly recognizable and infinitely more attractive; for a facelift is greatly needed if the institutional and political framework of contemporary Britain is not increasingly to be called into question. Moreover, all these criticisms have a great deal to do with Britain's failure to modernize and compete economically. Our economic failures are the consequence of a political system evolved in the nineteenth and early twentieth century. Cosmetic changes are not enough and the emphasis on Parliament in the media, when power lies elsewhere, is ironical. The civil servants, leaders of giant corporations and Trade Unions must be laughing with the key Ministers as they retain real power and simultaneously block the wheels of industrial and political progress.

CHAPTER TEN

Political and Structural Development

The House of Commons is taking the first tentative steps towards adapting to the changing needs of open government in the 1980s. But will the inertia of the past give way to a sensitive and responsive form of Executive behaviour in the future? This depends not only on Westminster. It is related to such matters as our electoral system, the political parties themselves and other institutions outside created to safeguard the rights of the ordinary citizen.

The changes at Westminster may well be a reflection of a wider desire for change. We have seen, for example, the growth of community politics, of law centres and similar media for channelling advice and protest in an extra-Parliamentary context. The ossification of the Parliamentary process gave rise to demands for other institutions to fill the gaps in procedures that did not appear to protect the victims of injustice and the under-privileged. The introduction of the Ombudsman, or Parliamentary Commissioner for Administration, was significant in this context, but, having served on the Standing Committee, I am all too well aware of the narrow ambit of his responsibilities and powers. Amendments not acceptable to the Government, which would have widened the scope of his powers were killed on the Report Stage. The creation of the Ombudsman is a welcome safeguard against maladministration and a step forward; but in its present form it is a tentative and cautious step. The time has come to review his powers which should go far beyond Ministries into the whole area of public service and enterprise.

Similarly, the Equal Opportunities Commission recognizes that women are to a large degree second-class citizens notwithstanding the emergence of a woman Prime Minister from among the nineteen women M.P.s. The Commission for Racial Equality is a recognition of another group in society which needs special attention. In the long term the problems of such groups can only be solved by changes in attitudes, but legislation can itself assist in such changes. The Employment Protection Bill has extended the scope of Industrial Tribunals to take on a role well beyond the payments of redundancy and unfair dismissal provisions. Within and without the official institutions created by Parliament there is therefore a recognition that in an increasingly complex society Parliament of itself cannot cope, even if it modifies itself to extend control over the Executive. Perhaps for this reason many potential activists are finding new ways of expressing themselves in a nation which is almost the home of the pressure groups.

Labour's 1980 conference at Blackpool reflected not just a shambles and the exposure of the block vote as a blunt and undemocratic weapon whether wielded by right or left. It showed the intolerance of the totalitarian minded section of the left as well as the poverty of philosophy of the traditional right. The Electoral College proposal for the leadership is a symptom of genuine frustration by honest men at ill-conceived policies such as the 5% which preceded the winter of discontent and Labour's demise. It is also part of the effort by others who have no love for democracy and tolerance to dictate their views through tiny caucuses. If Labour were still the mass party of the past things would be different.

Today, so many parties are moribund or tiny groups of activists: so many union branches are attended by a miniscule minority of members that the votes attributed to both at Conference are a fiction. A dozen determined men could take over many a party with a little determination. A ballot of the total membership would be the nearest thing to democracy.

A primary system or P.R. would ensure representation of voters' real preferences prior to election.

The Electoral College is something of a nonsense. A Party leader must have the confidence of the M.P.s he leads and the Party in the country. Members are representatives not delegates albeit sometimes unrepresentative. To bring the whole Party into the process of electing a leader also presupposes a postal ballot and proper records of membership. A leader not endorsed by the whole membership nor by a majority of the Parliamentary Party but by an electoral college incorporating the block vote would not have any moral authority. It is merely a means of circumventing obstacles in the way of a particular possible candidate.

The failure of the 'Day of Action' in 1980 to mobilize the masses showed that Labour misread the traditional methods acceptable in this country where there is no entrenched tradition of industrial action for political ends. In many ways the Labour Party is moving further from its natural supporters. Its successes are based on the swing of the pendulum from unpopular Conservative administrations rather than massive enthusiasm. The Party is in debt at the time of writing and, a year after leaving the House, I am still waiting for someone to ask me for a subscription. Activists are few and the Party has at all times failed to capture the imagination of the radical and the young, with the possible exception of the Suez episode. As a vote-delivering machine it is more successful but even in that sphere there are unpleasant omens. Only the electoral system keeps its developing inner rift within the same quarrelsome whole although no one is better qualified than Michael Foot to preserve the unity of M.P.s and the broader Party as well as Trade Unions.

The Party was always prone to splits and ideological battles but as a broad church it was able to contain most of them. Those like the I.L.P. who went into the wilderness withered away. Newspapers have always predicted a fatal split between right and left and many made the most of the militant faction's influence. However this time, and in a more complex way than the simplistic analysis of the press suggests, the Party faces a very real crisis. The current rifts are somehow different in quality from those which preceded them. For the first time I recall there is a rift that is so deep that common interests may not prevent an open split by some members hastened by mandatory reselection. Sometimes the controversies were so central to political debate that even if they endangered electoral hopes they actually brought in members who wanted to be where the real battle was. Today, few can follow the machinations of different groups which elevate internal issues into major causes of dissent for more obscure causes. This theme is central to the disaffection I myself feel as after fifteen years I look from the outside into the Labour goldfish bowl.

If Labour is acting in a curious way it is in part a reaction to what has happened at the opposite pole, as well as its own failure to comprehend the changed environment in which it has to function. Thatcherism reflects the philosophy behind Sir Keith Joseph's recent publication *View of Equality*. It is a notion dismissed with compelling and frightening logic in his book of that name. If it is contended that a free-for-all ultimately leads to the public good we are facing a philosophy quite alien to the comparatively liberal era of Butler, Boyle or Edward Heath himself. This new Toryism is rigid, arrogant and divisive in a way that we have not seen since the 1930s. All the more reason therefore that one should ask why the opposition parties are not able to take advantage of this lurch to the right. The monetarist ideology which has created an unacceptable number of unemployed, combined with an unacceptable degree of inflation, is nonetheless accepted, even if that acceptance is one of unhappy resignation.

Sir Keith Joseph and Sir Geoffrey Howe can rightly point to the corporate accumulation of wealth and political power in so-called Socialist countries and to the danger of collectivism turning into totalitarianism. They conveniently ignore the vast concentrations of wealth in private corporations which are capable of toppling Governments and which are equally answerable to no one.

Perhaps the failure of both Parties is to detect the cynicism and alienation of those with little wealth and no power. Mr. Benn may not be the bogey man he is made out to be but there is a real fear that a revamped Labour Party may usher in the beginnings of totalitarianism. There is equally a growing suspicion of our current instruments of law and order that led to the death of Blair Peach, among other scandals. The ordinary citizen's personal freedom does not rank high on the list of priorities of the far left. For most Conservatives it does not exist at all other than in the economic sphere where it is elevated into a central dogma. The elector has little choice in relation to the brand of socialism or Toryism he prefers. The choice is limited to Thatcherism and a divided and confused Opposition.

In the context of this system the electorate sees little salvation from a Liberal Party, under-represented, curiously quiet, and lacking a coherent philosophy. Is Roy Jenkins lurking in the wings? Could Mr. Heath make a comeback? Is Mr. Healey a spent force? At the time of writing, these intangibles make the current scene of bitter division and confrontation subject to a possible change of scenario which exists only in the wishful thinking of political commentators. For the Liberal Party, and any other new alignments, are hemmed in by an electoral system which permits little flexibility or choice from within the current parties.

It is here that the growing support for a change in the electoral system could gain greater significance. Most favoured by the professional reformers is the single transferable vote. The Party slate, even on regional lines as proposed in relation to the European elections, could well strengthen existing bureaucracies and the apparatchiks. The German system which combines Constituencies with the latter is being looked at with interest. It is fairer in its total result, but combines the worst aspects of the unfairness of the first-past-the-post principle at Constituency level with the Party slate at Regional level.

I believe that the time has come to consider the electoral system itself. We have seen how, currently, we disenfranchise all but those living in about hundred Constituencies. Even that number is generously high. A tiny change of three in a hundred can swing the National pendulum from one party to its opponents. A minority of votes may give a majority of seats. There is no scope for the elector to choose the candidate he prefers or between candidates of the same Party. His choice is stark, and the falling percentage of electors using their votes may well reflect disenchantment with this limitation. The media turn the battle into a Presidential campaign, but this is only one reflection of Mr. Sedgemore's concept of Prime Ministerial Government.

The small caucus is elevated to a powerful force in each safe Constituency, hence the ferocious battle being waged on compulsory reselection and the entryism of the militant faction in the Labour Party. The current Party structure is ossified. Changing patterns of allegiance are frustrated. Minority views and smaller Parties may receive five or six million votes and be almost unrepresented. Smaller groups concentrated in one area such as Ulster Unionists or Scottish Nationalist may fare much better than those millions. Whatever else the system does, it cannot be defended as fair or truly representative.

Tom Ellis M.P. put this in perspective on behalf of the comparatively new and significant Labour Campaign For Electoral Reform:

'The weakness of Parliament is a direct consequence of the highly developed whipping system now capable of exercising its tyranny to such purpose that Parliament is in effect a rubber stamp endorsing the actions of the executive. There may be some intrepid individual Member who occasionally displays a wholly admirable independence of mind but they achieve little more than the minor irritation of political gadflies.'

He is right in emphasizing the gladiatorial nature of politics which we choose to term the two-party system. It is as artificial as the legal system where we often see a sophisticated game of cricket played by the rules rather than seeking after the truth. We present two alternatives and expect the jury to decide rather than trying to find out – as is frequently the case – whether the truth may lie in a different hypothesis from those presented by prosecution and defence.

Similarly, the adversary system in Parliament can distort reality. It may lead to each side scoring points by quoting what opponents said when they were in office or opposition. That is hardly a rational way of dealing with the rights and wrongs of an issue. It effectively swats the gadfly who tries to see beyond the battle of the moment or those of the past. The political prophet becomes a lonely eccentric. The independently minded becomes a stupid nuisance to whips interested in the mechanics rather than the issues. A whip's hat changes a politician's attitudes as surely as does a policeman's helmet. Individuality, originality and even integrity can be stifled or at least frowned upon from above with obvious consequences. The docile sheep who bleat aye or no in unison and follow their leaders into the lobbies can be rewarded in the fullness of time. All this preserves outmoded attitudes, and even those streams of thought which are well enough organized to participate in repeated rebellions have to work within the framework of a system which almost inevitably defeats them.

Those who do not entirely identify with the major political parties have to seek other ways of influencing the political process. In our increasingly complicated and stratified society, with its numerous pressure groups, an outmoded system based essentially on the battle between capital and labour is inadequate to reflect that diversity. There is an inherent over-simplification. The irony is that these countervailing pressures have come about because of the evolution of society in which radical economic and educational reforms of a Labour Government played a major part.

The former Cabinet Minister, Edmund Dell, once argued that such reforms can only come about within the context of our electoral system which gives one party an overall majority. (Significantly he recently joined the Society for Electoral Reform.) However, it does not necessarily achieve such a result, as 1974 twice proved. Or it may translate the majority of votes for the left into seats for the right, as in 1951. The real answer lies in looking outwards to the success of countries in Europe with diverse forms of proportional representation. In any event our compromises are less democratic and open to debate since they occur within broad political parties. They are no less compromises for that.

The compromises may not only be behind closed doors but,

as with the so-called Lib-Lab pact, made without prior electoral approval. In West Germany a voter not only knows that the Free Democrats will enter into a coalition with the Social Democrats, but he may encourage them over the five per cent threshold just in order to achieve that object. Parties can go into an election openly declaring their intentions, as Labour and Fine Gael did in Ireland. There the elector can choose not only the Party but the individual member, and he can number his preferences under the Single Transferable Vote system. Curiously, Labour introduced this into the Northern Ireland Elections but this system, which has worked so well over the water, has until recently hardly figured as a central issue in serious political debate. The efforts of Enid Lakeman and her colleagues of the Proportional Representation Society have been valiant. Liberal support has been put down to self-interest but no one in a position to initiate change seems to have looked at the interests of democracy itself.

Thus the Parliamentary scene is frequently a distortion of reality, unable to represent the diversity of views within society. Two monoliths containing strange bedfellows, plus a handful of Liberals and Nationalists and the Northern Ireland contingent, which is more unrepresentative than the rest, is clearly not what electorate would choose if the system allowed more freedom of choice. If that view is challenged, then the answer is to try it out, for there would be nothing to fear. The farcical and damaging story of the unfortunate Steel Industry stems from an ins-and-outs game based on the changed views of a tiny percentage of those who bother to vote.

Far from creating Governments based on shabby compromises, we would see more responsive Government; the open exposition of varying viewpoints; and greater concentration on constructive policies rather than opposition for its own sake. True, constituencies would be large under a system of proportional representation. Manchester might be a single Constituency returning its six or seven members. There would not be the absurd situation where in some cities no Tory voter is represented while in large areas of the South of England a Labour M.P. is an endangered species. There would be an end to the hypocrisy that seems to bracket Marxists with Liberals on the one side and racists with Liberals of a slightly bluer complexion on the other.

The electoral system at present is more the product of society than the instrument which shapes it. There is an interaction. Change might well stop the stultification of politics and reinvigorate political and Parliamentary life. Untapped sources of expertise and enthusiasm not conforming to established dogmas might make a significant contribution to new dimensions of thought. The ecologists are an example of such a group but there are many more. Labour, when it was the third minority Party, called for proportional representation as an essential principle of democratic government. Modern Liberals must deplore their short-sighted and self-interested forbears who resisted it.

Of course there are several models for proportional representation which make that subject a debate in itself but that is no reason in itself to differ with the self-evident statement once made by the Labour Party. New alignments would be inevitable, just as thousands of active people would be drawn from extra-Parliamentary pressure groups into a situation where Westminster may appear relevant. That will be even more so if the changes at Westminster materialize. By the same token they are more likely to materialize in the context of a different system.

The other major Constitutional change must surely be to end the unrepresentative anachronism of the House of Lords. The hours my colleagues and I wasted dealing with Lords Amendments proved two things: that there is a need for a second chamber to scrutinize the details of legislation as the last filter before passing into law; and that should be a small Chamber elected like the Irish Senate from the House or by the Electorate. It could take some of the workload from the Commons. It could use experience and expertise in examining legislation more critically than sometimes occurs in the lower House. However, its powers should be strictly limited and like every other institution it should be answerable to the Electorate. There is no reason why, on suitable Select Committees, its members should not sit as equals along with equally accountable Members of the Commons.

148

I also believe that the time has come to subsidize political parties in the interests of democracy. This does not buy them. It frees them from paymasters be they industrialists, press barons, Trade Unions or other already influential groups within society. Information would be freer, since parties could publish more in competition with the established press. Already anti-establishment groups like State Research or the more popular *Time Out* have shown the need for an alternative press. How the parties use their money will be their concern. It may be on television advertizing or on more research staff but it is an overdue reform and one which will again add to the independence of parties and Members of Parliament. Some of the full-time party staff could service M.P.s in research and information where there is at present a notable lack of liaison.

These thoughts on the reform of our institutions and the state of our major parties is based on fifteen years in the House and, it must be admitted, on previously held prejudices. However, those years and a period of reflection following them, have only strengthened the views that I came increasingly to hold over the last few years. Those views vitally concern the perception I now have of the Party I worked for as that ten-year-old boy in the halcyon days of 1945.

That these thoughts have evolved following the 1970 defeat can be seen by successive articles published in *Contemporary Review*. I sought to analyze Labour's failure to follow up its 1966 success in a context removed from traditional right-left divisions. I saw nothing 'left' in capitulating to the strong and hitting the weak over incomes policy which would be the result of a so-called left-wing free-for-all mirroring the ideas of Sir Keith Joseph. The so-called right, represented by Jim Callaghan, had little to offer in terms of tapping idealism and no one was willing to discuss the topic of the electoral system itself, even the group around Shirley Williams. After the inconclusive minority Labour Government of 1974 I articulated these thoughts in *Contemporary Review*:

It has always been conventional wisdom that Proportional Representation was the root cause of the fragmentation of political parties in countries with an inferior system. It was rarely if ever argued, although I have long suspected it, that the system of election is frequently a reflection of the divisions in society rather than its cause.

The other pillar of conventional wisdom in the major political parties was the need for firm government or, in the Labour context, the need for a clear majority to carry out fundamental changes in our economic structure. However, it is increasingly apparent that, in almost every democratic country where parties are based on interest groups and ideology, it has become progressively more difficult to form single party majority governments. Recent examples in the Scandinavian countries and the Benelux, the German Experience of the Centre left coalition and the mirror image of Golda Meir with her own internal difficulties after receiving about the same proportion of seats as Harold Wilson but under the P.R. Party slate system, may pose a fundamental question about the nature of the more advanced industrial nation in relation to its political structure.

It is not without significance that in an election (1970–4) where I personally experienced the most remarkable loyalty and unparalleled enthusiasm of the Party and Trade Union rank and file, Labour did no more than strengthen its grip on existing urban bastions and capture a few – some with the unsolicited help of Mr. Enoch Powell – that it had no right to lose in 1970. Its share of the vote was considerably lower than at any election in my lifetime. When the kissing has to stop and post-election euphoria wears off it will have to consider how it can become the natural party of power that it promised to be in 1966 – or alternatively whether there is an argument for a change in our electoral system to give expression to a new political phenomenon in complex industrial societies which had no commitment in one of the most divisive and polarised elections on record.

There is a new complexity in our geographical and class structure; there is a less stark confrontation in that vast area where the Liberals took second place. There is a greater sophistication in an electorate subjected to the media and more individualistic in its comparative affluence. There is above all a large segment of society whose roots have withered as the proportion of basic manual workers in society has declined. They are attracted by efficiency, consistency and logic rather than the gut policies upon which the recent election was fought. Whether the Labour Party can reach out to them with a fresh and radical approach to the problems that afflict our society without hitting them too hard financially is a challenge in respect of which we are not entirely in control.

If we cannot, then this vocal and articulate segment will become increasingly alienated from a system which denies it a voice and denies those in the major Parties who have some understanding of their attitudes – while not necessarily sharing them – the opportunity to create the dialogue by rendering them politically important.

Recently Anthony Wedgwood Benn has assumed the mantle of the leader of the left. His hostility to the E.E.C. is a development of past attitudes and accords with the feelings of a backward-looking rank-and-file unable to see that socialism and democracy do not stop at Dover. He appears to oppose an incomes policy notwithstanding the fact that small strategically placed groups can wield massive negotiating power while nurses and many shop floor workers have little industrial muscle. On the other hand he espouses the cause of Open Government and sees the false priorities of a society where weapons of destruction take priority over kidney machines. Mr. Callaghan understands the need for Government and trade union cooperation and is a realist in this sphere. By contrast, his conservatism, reflected in his entourage, is hardly an inspiration. If the former has unwittingly become a charming demagogue and the latter a skilful suvivor I must look elsewhere for inspiration.

To fuse a planned incomes policy and sometimes self-restraint with the idealism of those who see beyond the 1980s to underlying and horrific international trends may be asking for a miracle. Some people name Roy Jenkins as the man to lead us out of the wilderness. If so, it will have to be with the support of something more appealing and radical than the present Liberal Party revamped. Others look to Shirley Williams. Mr. Healey would no doubt carry on traditional poli-

151

cies but at least the acrobatics of the Wilson era have gone. It may well be a mistake, however, to look just for personalities. If there is sufficient demand for radical policies suited to the world we live in rather than the one we were born into, then personalities may emerge from broader movements. In the meantime disenchantment with the Party I represented does not erase a deep loyalty. Like an estranged lover one hopes for reconciliation and a new and deeper relationship. A change in institutions may well speed this. The alternative is the mixture as before, and a crusading Mr. Benn would be preferable to that, but Michael Foot's election reflects a yearning for a combination of radicalism and realism which has raised my hopes.

Meanwhile the Labour Party seems intent upon its internicine warfare. Electoral defeat breeds such responses and the issues of compulsory reselection, which Mr. Benn has nailed to his mast, was one of these. The day of action and attempted militancy in the face of Mrs. Thatcher's cuts in public services provided another test in socialist virility. But of all the irrelevant issues the greatest furore was over the infiltration of the 'militant' faction as if the phenomenon was new. The attitudes to the controversy provide nevertheless an interesting insight into the current divide and the way in which the minds of the two major factions work.

It was characteristic of John Wyndham's *The Midwich Cuckoos* that while apparently planted by some alien force they were nurtured in their host society and grew up sharing a common mind. A simplistic diagnosis of outside infiltration is as erroneous as the supposition in Wyndham's novel – that only ruthless destruction will suffice to eliminate the danger. The paranoid fear of a destructive left-wing is a sad development in what should be a mass Party. It also taints many genuine people with a Troskyist brush merely because some of their views coincide while the real fellow travellers play to the *Morning Star* reporter in the Press Gallery unscathed.

The hue and cry about the Militant faction within the Labour Party gave Fleet Street a field day. However, it was in itself neither new nor particularly newsworthy. Like all the other newly-scratched wounds that are festering in the Labour

Party, the injury is self-inflicted and, to a large degree, psychosomatic. Similar groups had as much, if not more, influence when I was active in the Young Socialists in the 1950s. Bans and proscriptions were thought necessary before and since. No one took much notice and the groups were consigned to Britain's political fringe as largely irrelevant.

The difference now is that the suppression of the so-called 'Underhill Report' has become a rallying cry for insecure right-wingers, while left-wingers can equally conveniently accuse their opponents of McCarthyism in initiating a witch-hunt. Both sides selected the issue as one on which to make a stand and thereby elevated it into something out of all proportion to its intrinsic importance. Its real significance lies in the willingness of entrenched Tribunite and Manifesto militants (with a small m) to enter into vigorous confrontation in the wake of electoral defeat after a fairly long period of relatively peaceful coexistence.

The majority of positions in the Young Socialists used to be held by supporters of the Socialist Labour League – now the Workers Party Revolutionary. Decorated by Vanessa Redgrave and led by Gerry Healy, the would-be British Lenin, this group existed under various guises before marching into the wilderness under its own scarlet colours. Frequently termed the League of Militant Psychopaths by its detractors, its main targets were the other less holy Marxist groups which also influenced fringe elements in the Labour Party.

One of these, the International Socialists, drew its inspiration from Rosa Luxemburg in rejecting the concept of a Vanguard Party. Its prophet, Tony Cliff, even wrote her biography and its latter-day devotees have played a prominent role in the formation of the Anti-Nazi League and emerged as the Socialist Workers Party. However, the most 'entryist' of these groups, loosely termed Marxist or Trotskyist, was the Fourth International faction which commanded support in Liverpool and Nottingham rather than in the scattered cells of the International Socialists and the extended tentacles of the 'Lavender Hill mob' in the Socialist Labour League. Indeed, the grand old Duke of Clapham, Gerry Healy, who marched his light brigade into the Labour Party and out again, attracted the cannon fire right, left, in front and behind. For no one hates the Trotskyists more than the most influential of all Marxists, the Soviet-orientated Communists and their fellow-travellers who also inhabit sections of the Labour Party and the Trade Union Movement.

The sudden discovery of these forces has more to do with Conference resolutions on compulsory re-selection and the dominance of Tony Benn's supporters on the National Executive than with any real change of circumstances. True, a few M.P.s are influenced by Militants, and it attracts the loyalty of committed Young Socialists. It is certainly strong in some big cities, but its real support is minimal compared to the other streams of thought in the Labour Movement. Like all such groups, it loses more of its Midwich Cuckoos to complete nervous political exhaustion and creeping respectability than it wins over to the coming revolution. It also has a positive influence in provoking relevant discussion, elevating theoretical and historical knowledge in a rather Philistine Party and in providing devoted workers in many a vacuum.

Were it as strong as alleged – in Manchester, for example, – then it is indeed strange that the latest three Parliamentarians from that area are respectable local Councillors cast in a rather pedestrian mould. True, such groups make up what they lack in numbers in – dare I say it? – militancy. The poverty of thought on the part of the right wing and the alienation of radicals from the Labour Party has left a vacuum. Were there a really radical alternative rather than a revamped Centre Party, the groundswell of support among the progressive and libertarian elements in Britain would swamp the Militants.

The latter are deeply rooted in factional, theoretical and indeed theological differences within the Communist movement, as Stalin gradually annihilated every opposition tendency within the Soviet Union in the 1930s. This is why its policies are an anachronism by half a century and why it cannot find any significant body of support by existing apart from the Labour Party. Its existence is less harmful than a witch hunt. The publication of the Underhill Report would be less harmful than the speculation and hysteria provoked by non-publication. Its tradition is as valid as the Christian Socialists, Social Democrats, Tribunites, Reformists and countless strands which together make up the British Labour movement. Ideas should be fought by better ideas and it is a slur on the intelligence of the Labour Party membership to suggest that these fringe groups can hoodwink them into creating a Marxist state.

Even posing the hypothesis of a well-orchestrated Militant take-over, it would then be open to the opponents of the group to divide and challenge them in an open combat, the result of which is hardly at issue. Where local Parties become rotten boroughs and the opportunist politics of expediency, typified by the Wilson epoch, have provoked cynicism, these Militant or other similar groups have been provided with ideal conditions for development. Genuine Tribunites or Manifesto group members would do better to argue about objects, policies and strategies for the eighties rather than indulge in a mud-slinging battle that does credit to neither, and damages the Labour Party as a whole.

Sensationalism on the one hand and a failure to acknowledge the reality of a well-documented phenomenon on the other are equally unbalanced reactions. There are enough demons to exorcise in the shape of Sir Keith Joseph or the invaders of Afghanistan, without becoming obsessed by small groups of dissident Marxists who have yet to gain the influence obtained by the Communist Party in the Trade Unions and elsewhere. In any event, they provoke similarly intemperate attacks by Militant on the so-called moderate wing of the Party, branded as middle-class infiltrators by the guardians of Socialist purity attracted to these sectarian groupings.

In grasping an understanding of the decline of freedom in the Soviet Union and in broadening an otherwise insular approach to politics; in stimulating a near-religious zeal among idealistic young people, the Militant group performed a service. That much of its subsequent analysis of world events is grotesquely distorted and that disillusion may lead those same people to apathy is a balancing factor of no little significance but a risk libertarians and democrats should face in open political debate. Indeed, the most significant factor in these sectarian groupings is their high turn-over – life expectancy usually being about three years.

There are other ironies about the situation. Tony Benn calls for open government, yet opposed publication of the evidence. Militant itself is the opposite of libertarian, with attitudes to vital social questions that make Mary Whitehouse appear permissive. The liberty it demands to organize within the Labour Party is strictly denied to those who join it. Indeed, the theological divide between its leader, Ted Grant, and the rival Healyites was based on a schism in International Trotskyism. The forerunners of Militant favoured the entry tactic, and great world-shaking noises were made between those who favoured the F.L.N. or the M.N.A. in Algeria. Similar divisions on the Middle East, the Anti-Nazi League or the nature of the Soviet Union permeated the internecine struggle of these groups.

In a sense, they mirror the factionalism of the far right, but if the Tories can tolerate a Bow Group or a Monday Club then, in spite of the highly organized and disciplined structure, the Militant group can be tolerated by a healthy Labour Party. The problem is that the Labour Party is not healthy and has failed to tap the latent discontent and radicalism among young people disenchanted with the existing political establishment.

The puritanical and out-dated slogans of those who argue that the Soviet Union is a 'degenerated Workers' State', requiring critical support, and those who dub it 'State Capitalist', like Tony Cliff, hardly create the sorts of debate likely to attract massive interest. Only when they batten on an existing campaign in a parasitical fashion do they attract any widespread sympathy. Nevertheless, I have a sneaking affection for their simplistic and idealistic clinging to an ideological purity that harks back to the golden age of good causes, when black and white were more recognizable than they are today.

This explains the attraction of Militant for devoted young socialists and by the same token fails to inspire the mass of young people more likely to participate in broadly based movements like the Anti-Nazi League, Rock Against Racism or, in its heyday, the Campaign for Nuclear Disarmament.

Patrick Wintour, writing in the *New Statesman*, has the merit of challenging Militant upon its methods and policies rather than upon administrative methods. After all, constituency take-overs are not unknown by strange forces in Islington or elsewhere; while Labour M.P.s have been known to act as P.R. men for Franco, the Greek Colonels or King Hussein of Jordan and to receive payment for it. In such a broad party, these aberrations, painful as they are, may be inevitable.

The one sure way of bringing these divisions into the open is as I have indicated, to change the electoral system to one where all such differences would face one another across the ballot box. Voters could express real preferences rather than choosing between, say, a Tribunite Socialist and a member of the Monday Club or a Jenkinsite and a liberal Tory or, indeed, any other permutation of two opponents. Nonetheless, the subject of electoral reform remains taboo among those in safe seats, propped up by weighty majorities.

Curiously, the sectarianism and self-made isolation of Militant is a more potent force in its destruction than a thousand reports on its activities. It remains a faction within a faction as the Labour Party Young Socialists holds its tiny 4,000 faithful and the Party's active support is slowly eroded, like the French socialists of the 1960s. It poses a minimal threat to the Labour Party, and the concern expressed by Labour's opponents is not only touching but counter-productive. The way to counter a once revolutionary and now irrelevant philosophy is to up-date one's own thinking and propagate it in an intelligent and attractive fashion.

The Labour Party will not solve its problems by a witch hunt directed at those propagating ideas that have never attracted the Labour Movement, let alone the general public. It will solve its problems when it recognizes the realities of 1980 rather than 1930 and puts forward solutions to the problems raised by the complexities of our modern inter-dependent industrial society. If ideas can only be defended by better ideas, the better ideas will have to be produced by careful analysis and thought. That is the task for those who currently prefer to throw mud at N.E.C. meetings rather than get out from their self-imposed political ghetto. Whether La-

bour will break out of that ghetto is the major question for
the 1980s. The outlook remains bleak unless Mrs. Thatcher
provides the stimulus. Both Anthony Wedgwood Benn and
Shirley Williams claim to have the key. The movement by
Benn's supporters to control Councillors is superficially democratic. In each case however, be it compulsory reselection,
policy making by the National Executive or the Election of
the leader, the so called democratization does not bring in the
mass of supporters or members but rather reinforces the Party
caucus which by its very nature is not representative of ordinary people and their aspirations. It is élitist. Of course
power wielded by M.P.s is also élitist in another way but
they are answerable to the total electorate. The answer is not
simple, and only by the reappraisal of the electoral system
and the Party structure as a whole can one resolve the dilemma. I believe Michael Foot understands this.

The suspicion is that all these arguments are about personal
ambition rather than principle. In the summer of 1980 the
so-called 'gang of the three' and so-called left wing missed
those more fundamental issues notwithstanding some sound
sense by the former. Only by their inability to see the futility
and danger of Cruise Missiles in contradiction to the rest of
their 'Manifesto'. Interestingly Callaghan and Healey seemed
less interested in ideology and almost embarrassed by a battle
of ideas. They represent a very significant section historically
of a movement for which pragmatism has traditionally been
more important than ideology, in contrast to its continental
counterparts.

CHAPTER ELEVEN

The Fringe, the Fight, the Frustration

In *The Secret Constitution*, Brian Sedgemore cites frightening examples of secrecy by cabinet committees and stone-walling by Ministers over vital questions of finance, industry and energy. Heads of industry and finance are shown to be party to a form of Government which hides the truth not only from the electorate but from M.P.s. My central interests in Parliament were very different – human rights, civil liberties and such esoteric topics as pseudo-religious cults and South African intelligence in Britain.

For several years between 1965 and 1969, virtually half my time was taken up in an attempt to warn Ministers and the public of the impending explosion in Northern Ireland. Of course, my interests were wide and various, but where I could claim some expertise I found the same stone wall, the same resistance to change, the same secrecy and even double-dealing on the part of Ministers who claimed to be personal friends. This was particularly so in the Home Office, corresponding to Mr. Sedgemore's experience in Energy. I did not experience it as P.P.S. to Mrs. Castle but that Ministry's work is not so delicate. The route of a ring road is not as vital to the nation as sanction busting in Rhodesia or the future of Ulster.

Nevertheless, the sensitivity of Government departments to any intrusion upon their domain is the greatest single cause for concern by those who consider open Government to be an essential element in a democracy. It was perhaps my own self-made difficulty that the political fringe fascinated me.

Together with American, South African and British journalists I investigated what I could of the activities of South African Intelligence in Britain. Some of the evidence had previously found its way to Jim Wellbeloved M.P. Although he was later a Minister, and although my files were sent to both the Prime Minister and the Home Secretary, I have no idea whether they were interested and know of no action taken. Curiously, this side of my activities, playing the private detective, gave me a great deal of pleasure. It put pressure, however, on personal relations at home and led to a good deal of scorn and incredulity outside, for intelligent people who know of Watergate become sceptics when they hear of anything similar in Britain.

Thus, I discovered unacceptable evidence of forgeries, bribery and atempts to damage the reputations of politicians in Britain. Some of this is documented beyond any doubt. Some may never be proven either way. The fact of the existence of these activities has now been confirmed by the Muldergate scandal. During our investigations, an attempt was made to enter my own house while I was at the home of a contact from Zimbabwe telephoning the wife of one of our sources of information in South Africa. Later, an ingenious entry was made into the flat of a girl who transcribed tapes secured by the same Mark Hosenball who was to be deported by Merlyn Rees for an unspecified reason. The fascinating aspect of the latter break-in was that nothing was taken although valuable stereo equipment and other items were in the flat. The girl was a non-political secretary. The only way our rendezvous could have been known was by a tapped telephone – either mine or the lady's from Zimbabwe, a white Rhodesian who had sympathies with the P.L.O. As some of the information concerned the alleged framing of Peter Hain on a bank robbery charge, we all subsequently visited him. Peter Hain himself is still doubtful that the matter had anything to do with South Africa and in spite of two statements from persons who allegedly saw relevant documents I must remain agnostic on that matter. One statement I took in the presence of a solicitor. Subsequently that solicitor's premises were broken into. When I saw the film of *All the President's Men* I had a feeling of *déjà vu* and my main worry was whether B.O.S.S. or our own intelligence was involved.

In view of evidence I had from a source close to M.I.5. I have no doubt that, in spite of our alleged antipathy to apartheid, the two organizations frequently worked together. Certainly, the late Peter Gladstone Smith, took the view that M.I.5. had a dossier on the South African plot to discredit British politicians and Members of the Liberal Party in particular. He was a brilliant crime reporter for the *Sunday Telegraph*, whose death, following Mark Hosenball's deportation, meant that the small coterie of 'investigators' with whom I worked on the activities of the far right was all but destroyed. When my most frequent informant took a job in the media it was the end of an era in which we had exposed some frightening phenomena on Britain's neo-Nazi wing.

All too often, one had to face the scoffing, sneering and ignorant antagonism of people who thought such things impossible, I remember receiving information from an Editor on a plot to blow up an El Al airliner at London Airport. One Labour M.P., who was virtually a public relations officer for Jordan, described the allegation in a not too pleasant manner. Ultimately the man responsible, a former Mosleyite who had been to Egypt, received a five-year sentence. Such naïvite may have given way to nervousness in the wake of more recent outrages involving diplomats, terrorists and fanatics. It was the same supercilious (or perhaps not disinterested) reaction which I received in attempting to warn the Government over Northern Ireland in 1965, or the horrendous activities of various organizations, whether political or pseudo-religious cults, a decade later. Whether its resistance is bred from scepticism, lethargy, sympathy induced by subtle bribery or their own convictions, the political establishment, guided by its civil service, will seldom move unless its hand is forced. There are also nasty consequences for those who push too hard.

On the South African issue I employed a thoroughly reliable assistant to collate my information, to interview those concerned wherever possible, but not to bother with the plot against the Liberal Party which had received adequate attention and on which I have a thick file. It is only partially conclusive without certain key documents, but is frightening to those who think that spy novels are no more than fiction dreamed up by imaginative writers. This file has never been published. Certain journalists have occasionally had access to parts of it. Some information was volunteered by a South African expatriate initially giving a false name over the telephone with whom I made a rendezvous. Of course the technique is to arrive nearby and overlook the spot to avoid a set-up. In fact her information on a former B.O.S.S. agent tallied with what I later learned from an entirely unconnected source. It included a photograph of him with a Liberal Peer and Lord Brockway at an anti-apartheid rally. To this day the lady in question has fears. I also had to use slightly unorthodox methods in order to obtain some of my information. The great advantage was the teamwork of mediamen and Parliamentarians which meant that between us we could verify one anothers' sources and the M.P. could then make public what ought to be public knowledge and inform the correct Minister of what was genuine security. That the latter information seemed swallowed into oblivion gives me cause for concern, not least when genuine investigatory journalists are pilloried, charged under the Official Secrets Act or deported. It seems that M.P.s and journalists should keep their noses clean, go through the right lobbies or even supplement page three of the Sun. But they should not step upon the preserves of our unknown protectors and rulers.

Since it is now history and makes remarkable reading for those unfamiliar with the political underground with which the probing politician may have to deal, I have printed for the first time in this book that part of my dossier which does not involve the alleged plot against Thorpe, Hain, Cyril Smith and other Liberals which we were investigating before. It was during that investigation that we came up against break-ins and tapped telephones and ultimately reached what appeared to be a dead end. (My experience of other issues however is that no doubt a day will come when some beans will be spilled and the truth known.) On this occasion I had the support of Harold Wilson and, after one radio interview he collared me in the lobby and, as an obvious hint, told me there would be a Government reshuffle. He clearly had a special interest in discrediting South African and also German sources for reasons best known to him. It may have something to do with the fact that one of my collaborators, from a well known American magazine, visited me in my room in the Commons after a visit to Germany.

This man refused to speak. He wrote down the name of a man who is now in the House of Lords linking him with Wilson. I said I knew of him. He indicated he no longer wanted any part in the investigations because of something he had seen in the files of an equally well known West German magazine. It was he who, with no difficulty, had given me the location and telephone number of my contact from Zimbabwe whose involvement I had only gleaned from a careful reading of the newspaper files. I assume he had C.I.A. contacts. She had been prepared to see me because she knew of my opposition to B.O.S.S. from the press. I had my own way of checking her trustworthyness and, although we differed in our attitudes on many things – Leila Khaled and Countess Marceiwitz were her heroines – she was a remarkable woman, as the following story of espionage reveals.

In December 1971, a group of Labour and Liberal M.P.s, led by James Wellbeloved, sent a dossier to the then Home Secretary, Reginald Maudling, giving details of an alleged BOSS inspired spy ring. In May 1967 an Englishman called Norman Blackburn had been arrested along with a Cabinet Office typist, Helen Keenan, and sentenced to 5 years imprisonment for passing Cabinet secrets to Rhodesia; these included minutes of discussions on the Beira pipeline in Rhodesia. These documents had been passed on to Blackburn's 'controller' in the Southern African intelligence service, who was at the time located in Brussels.

Norman Blackburn went to Rhodesia in 1960 and joined the Rhodesian army. In 1963 he was recruited in Bulawayo into the security service by John Fairer-Smith (then an officer in the Rhodesian Special Branch) working initially as his bodyguard. The job went on to entail checking on Rhodesians in the interests of the 'internal security' of the country.

In 1966 Blackburn came to England to continue his intelligence work for Fairer-Smith, using a series of casual jobs as a cover for this. He earned approximately £200 per month which he received in cash directly from Fairer-Smith (who was himself now based in England). From 1967 he received his money from a Mr. Kruger at South Africa House. His brief was to infiltrate any African organization, to recruit informers and to carry out other tasks of surveillance. Blackburn claimed to have had ten informers in different organizations. He also claimed that there were approximately seventy South African agents operating in England at this time.

Blackburn himself was in charge of operations in about six organizations. For instance, in January 1966 he joined ZAPU, posing as an African sympathizer. From ZAPU he obtained information on the African guerilla movements, on ZAPU sympathizers, etc. He obtained information on ANC activities also and on who was being paid to smuggle their literature into South Africa.

Blackburn also checked on South Africans and Rhodesians studying in England who were unsympathetic to their respective governments. This in fact appears to have been the emphasis of Blackburn's work. Among those under his surveillance were an Edinburgh schoolteacher, Margaret Clarke, who had previously been deported from Rhodesia, Oliver Read, a university lecturer, and Judy Todd, daughter of Garfield Todd, who was apparently under constant surveillance. Rooms of such people were bugged. According to Blackburn, Fairer-Smith had files on over 300 individuals in his flat. (This was later corroborated by another of Fairer-Smith's agents, Mohammed Childs, of whom more later.)

Blackburn and Fairer-Smith saw each other quite frequently and often drank together at the Playboy Club and at the Zambesi Club in Earls Court, a well known haunt of Rhodesians and South Africans. According to Blackburn, Fairer-Smith's money came from the South African government. Fairer-Smith also had dealings on the continent and would visit it at least twice a month. The spy network apparently operated in Scandinavia too.

At Blackburn's trial, the name of his controller was not mentioned and no action was taken against him although Blackburn did give the police detailed information about Fairer-Smith's activities. Again according to Blackburn, the activities of Fairer-Smith were already well known to the British intelligence service.

A few more facts about Fairer-Smith's background – until 1965 Fairer-Smith had been a detective sergeant in the British South Africa police (the Rhodesian police force). In 1965 he came to England, ostensibly as export manager for a company called Thermal Developments Ltd. Although Fairer-Smith's activities were not publicly exposed until 1971 with the collation of the dossier by the group of M.P.s, a 1969 pamphlet by an exiled P.A.C. official and writer, Mathew Nkoana, titled *Crisis in the Revolution*, had claimed that Fairer-Smith's flat in Chester Square, London, contained personal files on 250 people involved in liberation movements in Southern Africa and also technical equipment used in his espionage activities. (This was also claimed by Mohammed Childs.) Nkoana claimed that the spy network that Fairer-Smith had set up operated on behalf of all the white governments of Southern Africa.

In 1967 Fairer-Smith went to Johannesburg and on his return went into the 'credit ratings' business. Argen, a private detective agency, was registered in August 1968, Fairer-Smith and his wife being the sole directors. Argen conducted economic and political espionage in the U.K. and on the continent. By 1969 Argen was doing a lot of work for Gramco, and Fairer-Smith was responsible for circulating a lot of the early doubts about I.O.S. He was also the first man to reveal Jerry Hoffman's background in the U.S. – one of the effects of which was the resignation from the Hoffman group of Reginald Maudling in September 1969. One of the operations that Fairer-Smith set up on behalf of Gramco in Geneva, led to the arrest and trial of two of Fairer-Smith's operatives on charges of illegal bugging.

It has been possible to establish the identities of other of Fairer-Smith's operatives in England at this period and I have collected a full dossier on these.

One is a man by the name of Eli Stalmans, a Belgian, whose father was an engineer in South Africa, and who worked in London on the business section of the journal *Africa and the World*.

Another operative was an Englishman called Mohammed Childs. Childs, an active supporter of P.A.C., was recruited through Stalmans. Childs and Stalmans had both been working on the journal *Africa and the World*.

Another man who seemed to be working for South African Intelligence at this period and whose work has been linked with that of Fairer-Smith's was a South African called Keith Wallace. Wallace died in unexplained circumstances in London in 1970.

He was found dead in a well outside his bedroom window by three friends who had been searching for him, worried, in view of his disturbed state of mind, that he had not been seen for three days. Wallace often used to enter his flat through this window after climbing out to it from the landing when he forgot his keys, and despite contradictory pieces of evidence, the inquest recorded a verdict of accidental death while trying to climb in the window. When the police were first called and were shown signs of disarray in the flat – the doorhandle of his room was bent as if forced, there were four small bloodstains on the curtains and two pieces of panelling from the bed were on the floor – they said they would be basing their investigations on these items of evidence. However after consultation with their colleagues, they decided not to investigate further.

In addition to the evidence above, it was discovered that several of Wallace's belongings were missing. These included his revolver, which he always carried in his shoulder holster, a wristlet tape recorder and his wallet containing his identity and press cards.

Another agent named by Childs was a man called Hans Lombard. An extensive documentation of his activities is to be found in Nkoana's pamphlet *Crisis in the Revolution*, where he describes Lombard as a 'lone operator concerned with the whole of Africa', by contrast with the Fairer-Smith organization which was concerned with the whole of Southern Africa.

An Afrikaner, Lombard came to England in 1958, describing himself as a 'freelance writer, journalist and photographer' and an opponent of apartheid. Until 1958. Lombard worked as a journalist on *Die Vaderland*, a Johannesburg daily, once edited by Verwoerd. He was remembered by South African exiles for the part he played during a police raid on a multi-racial party at the Johannesburg home of a Communist lawyer, Joe Slovo. The party was to celebrate the release of a large number of prisoners from the Treason Trials. Lombard gatecrashed this party and during the raid climbed on to a table and took photographs. After the raid, police came to *Die Vaderland* asking for information on the party. According to Lombard, he refused to give any and this led to his losing his job and his leaving South Africa for good. Lombard told another story to explain his departure from South Africa – this was that he had been having an affair with an African girl and he was afraid of being prosecuted under the Immorality Act.

When he came to England, Lombard went to live in Slough where he worked for about two years on the *Windsor, Slough and Eton Express*. We worked briefly in 1961 on the *South London Advertiser* as a junior reporter (although Lombard later claimed that he had been the paper's deputy editor). He met Fenner Brockway M.P. and 'became close friends with him and gave him a lot of valuable information to use in the House of Commons on South Africa'. Questioned about this claim in 1969, Brockway said that he had no recollection of this and described Lombard as 'a rather brash young man who appeared suspiciously keen to ingratiate himself'.

In 1962 Lombard appeared at P.A.C. headquarters in Maseru with a letter of introduction from Brockway and soon became accepted as trustworthy by the P.A.C. leader, Potlako Leballo. He was given a P.A.C. assignment in the Transkei and was, rather surprisingly, successful in obtaining a visa to enter the region. White people were usually refused permission to enter the Transkei. During the assignment he visited P.A.C. underground cells, met activists, saw arms caches. His companion, Leballo's aid Mgaju, was arrested and imprisoned soon after their return. Meanwhile Lombard continued his travels, with a further letter of credentials from Mgaju. Early in 1962 he was in London and was then heard of in Ghana and South Africa, appearing in P.A.C's London office towards the end of 1962. In 1963 he attended a conference of the Afro-Asian People's Solidarity Organization where he made contact with S.W.A.P.O. activists. He left there for Dar-es-Salaam where he learnt of the movements of the first P.A.C. military trainees and of two senior P.A.C. officials. Very shortly afterwards these two were arrested in Rhodesia. Lombard was meanwhile travelling around Southern Africa, supposedly in pursuit of news. None of his dispatches were ever seen.

In March 1963 Lombard returned to Maseru and obtained a strongly-worded testimonial from Leballo which described Lombard as 'a true dedicated fighter for African freedom in the P.A.C. ranks'. Lombard made frequent journeys between Maseru and Johannesburg. After one trip to South Africa, he warned Leballo of an impending police raid on P.A.C. offices during which many important documents were to be seized. Thanks to this tip-off, Leballo escaped imprisonment.

Lombard's association with the liberation movements was not confined to that with P.A.C. He also worked to gain the confidence of S.W.A.P.O. However, the only known article that he wrote in support of the liberation movements was that published in *Peace News*, in approximately mid-1963. And his work with P.A.C. enabled him to collect very valuable information on the individuals and on the strategy of the liberation movements.

Lombard maintained a flat in Earls Court for use on his frequent visits to London. He kept varied company in London. He mixed with African activists and diplomats, often throwing lavish parties. He was often seen at diplomats' parties. He was also once seen in the company of the South African Minister of Defence during the latter's visit to London.

In 1966 he made contact with Sam Nujoma, president of S.W.A.P.O., who was in the Hague for a case being brought by African states against South Africa on the question of South West Africa in the International Court of Justice. Nujoma was due to come to London and Lombard offered to book a hotel room for him, which he did. The day after Nujoma's arrival in England, Lombard invited him to a party at his flat. While the party was in progress, Nujoma's hotel room was raided and his briefcase, which contained important and confidential documents, was removed. No valuables were taken. Some time later, at the trial of thirty-seven South West African patriots in Pretoria, a letter from Nujoma to the Commander-in-Chief of S.W.A.P.O's liberation forces, which had been written just after judgement had been delivered at the Hague, was one of the items produced in evidence by the prosecution.

From 1967 to 1969 Lombard, now back in South Africa, was political editor of the pro-government *Financial Gazette*. In 1968 he wrote in support of the government's Bantustan policy for the Transkei, contradicting his previous posture of opposition to this. He also wrote in support of Vorster's counter insurgency exercises. This is the same man who, as Nkoana bitterly pointed out, was described by Leballo as a leading freedom fighter.

Lombard denies that he was ever a spy. He has attempted to explain his extensive knowledge of the liberation movements and of so many of their activists as resulting from his 'criss-crossing Africa as a journalist'. As Nkoana remarked: 'the extent and volume of the intelligence amassed by Lombard over the years must be staggering'. Nkoana blamed Leballo for throwing the field wide open to Lombard and accused him of being totally negligent as regards security.

Another freelance operator collecting information for use by the South African authorities was the journalist Gordon Winter. Winter, a Yorkshireman by birth, left England in 1968 where he had engaged in various dubious activities including, allegedly, male prostitution and gun-running. He was involved with the Richardson gang who were then operating in South Africa (Winter's wife, Jean Lagrange later married Charles Richardson) and in 1968 became incriminated in a murder case and was subsequently deported to

England. While in South Africa Winter worked for the Johannesburg black weekly *Drum* whose editor, Cecil Eprile, was later to come to London as chief editor on Forum World Features. Winter mainly wrote gossipy stories for *Drum* but drew some attention to himself with a scoop interview he did with Nelson Mandela in jail the day after Sharpeville. There were some questions as to why the security authorities would have set this up for him.

On his arrival in England, Winter claimed that he had been deported for political reasons. He also claimed that he had been running refugees across the border while in South Africa. When he left Johannesburg, his flat was found to contain several items of electronic equipment.

He worked in England as a freelance journalist, becoming secretary of the London freelance branch of the N.U.J. He wrote for a new agency called Forum World Features, whose chairman was Brian Crozier (now running the Institute for the Study of Conflict) and whose chief editor was Winter's former associate in South Africa, Cecil Eprile. Forum supplied several articles each week to 150 newspapers in fifty countries. Winter also sold stories from time to time to South African newspapers.

He became a very familiar figure to those in London involved in Southern African liberation movements. He attended demonstrations, took photographs, offered information. He often supplied A.A.M. with photographs of demonstrations. At one particular anti-apartheid demonstration he was asked why he was only taking photographs of South African exiles and replied that they might prove useful should he ever want to get back to South Africa. He was constantly trying to gain the confidence of officials of A.A.M. and often went into their offices. He posed as an African sympathizer although it seems that there was a tacit acceptance on both sides that he was supplying the South African authorities with information. He also constantly worked on gaining the confidence of other South African patriots and kept detailed dossiers on each of them. He wrote articles for the South African newspapers on several of them causing considerable distress and danger. Winter attended all the Stop the Seventies Tour demonstrations, again taking many photographs. He later appeared for the prosecution in Peter Hain's trial and told a friend that he did it solely so that it would do him credit in the eyes of the South African authorities. At the time of the exposé in English newspapers of working conditions in South Africa, Winter was paid very handsomely by a South African newspaper to go to Hong Kong to do a story on corruption and exploitation in English companies there, and was told that this would help him to return to South Africa too.

Winter shared a flat from 1969 to 1971 with Murray Llewellyn, director of a language school, and Jill Evans, a fashion writer on the Daily Mirror. In 1976 Llewellyn wrote that he was 'quite convinced that he was in the employ or at any rate pay of B.O.S.S.'. Winter was seen as something of a journalistic prostitute, 'completely and utterly without any scruple or conscience, especially when monetary gain was involved', and as such it seems unlikely that the South Africans would have had any need to put him on their payroll. There is only one case in which Winter acted openly in the interests of the South African authorities. This occurred in connection with the exposure of the activities of the Christopher Robert agency when the journalist involved in writing the story was threatened by Winter and others.

Lee Tracy, a professional 'bugger', and freelancer for English intelligence, who knew Winter in London, says that he did jobs for Winter. He also claims that Winter was leant on by MI6 and had to leave England. For whatever reason, in 1974 Winter returned to South Africa, the first deportee to have been allowed to return. He is now working there as chief reporter for the Johannesburg Sunday Express.

In March 1976 Norman Scott revealed that Winter had tried to sell the story of his allegations about Thorpe to a British Sunday newspaper in July 1971. At the end of 1975 Winter wrote to Scott from South Africa suggesting he come to South Africa as soon as possible where Winter would break the story about Thorpe.

In November 1968 Ian Withers admitted that his detective agency, the Christopher Robert Agency, had investigated the activities of the A.A.M. and the private lives and activities of its supporters, and that agents had covered the London hearing of the U.N. Special Committee on apartheid which met in July 1967. It was also discovered that the agency had investigated 'John Lawrence' (the pseudonym of a South African exile who had written a book entitled *Seeds of Disaster*, which details the methods used in South African government propaganda). The head of Amnesty's African department was also investigated by the agency. (Withers denied these latter cases but there seems no doubt that the agency did undertake the investigation.)

One of Withers' agents, Channon Wood, who apparently was the source of the disclosure of their spying on A.A.M., was found dead two and a half months later on Wimbledon Common.

Over the past fifteen years, there has been a series of burglaries carried out on the homes and premises of both Africans and English people involved in some way, however tenuous, in opposition to apartheid. What has led to links being made between burglaries which might have seemed unconnected and perhaps coincidental in terms of their victims is the fact that usually no material valuables have been taken. Flats and offices have been ransacked, confidential documents have been removed and more obvious items have been ignored. In some cases, stolen documents have reappeared as prosecution evidence in trials back in South Africa.

In 1963, documents were stolen from the P.A.C. office in Grand Buildings, London. Some of these later reappeared at the trial in the same year in South Africa of the Rev. Arthur Bleixall.

In 1966, the hotel room in London of Sam Mujoma, President of S.W.A.P.O., was burgled while he was attending a party given by Hans Lombard. A briefcase containing important documents was removed.

In 1967, the A.A.M. reported a break-in to their offices. Two drawers of used stencil skins, all the subscription cards and the bulk order book for their newspaper were removed.

In 1969 there was a break-in at the S.W.A.P.O. offices in Oxford Street, shortly after the arrival in England of the new

S.W.A.P.O. representative, Peter Katjavivi. Nothing was taken.

In 1971 the telephone book of the executive secretary of A.A.M., Ethel de Keyser, disappeared from the offices. The book contained telephone numbers of M.P.s, press contacts, South Africans, etc.

In 1971 both Amnesty and I.D.A.F. reported burglaries.

In December 1971, a burglary occurred at the Society of Friends Peace Committee Offices in London when a general file was taken as well as a file containing information on the visits of South Africans to Britain and the subscription cards to the Peace Committee.

In July 1972, Alexandre Moumbaris and his wife were arrested in South Africa under the terms of the Terrorism Act. While in prison, Mrs. Moumbaris was shown some photos and documents which could only have originated from their flat in London. After four months detention, Mrs. Moumbaris was released and flown to Paris where she discovered that in August 1972 a man had been to see her mother-in-law, introducing himself as a friend of Moumbaris, with a letter supposedly from Alexandre asking her to give the key of their London flat to this man. In September, Mrs. Moumbaris' parents and her mother-in-law, worried that they had had no news of their children, went to London where they found that the flat had been ransacked. At Moumbaris's trial, the prosecution produced in evidence papers which were among those stolen from the flat.

In November 1973, Astrid Winer, the coloured wife of a detained white South African photographer, complained of B.O.S.S. harassment. It appeared that her London flat had been broken into and searched, that she had been followed, that her phone had been tapped, and that the flats of two friends she had visited were broken into shortly after she had visited them.

In September 1975 an A.N.C. member, Shanti Naidoo, who had been under detention in South Africa and had come to England in 1972, found the house that she shared with her sister and brother-in-law had been broken into and ransacked. Nothing was removed but all their papers had been examined.

In April 1975 the flat of the General Secretary of S.A.C.-T.U. and chairman of the London branch of A.N.C., John Gaetswe, was broken into and ransacked while he was away in Canada. Other members of A.N.C. have also reported break-ins. There was one in 1974 and again in 1975 at the home of Billy Nannan, chairman of A.N.C's Youth Section and another at the home of Herby Pillay, secretary of the London branch of A.N.C.

In February 1975, S.W.A.P.O's spokesman at the U.N., Ben Gurirab had his Bloomsbury hotel room burgled. Letters and documents were stolen.

In 1975, a former detainee, Ms Ramnie Dinat found her London home had been burgled. Her papers had been examined. Nothing was taken.

In 1975, S.W.A.P.O's representative in London, Peter Katjavivi, discovered a prowler at this home.

In 1975, S.W.A.P.O. offices in Tabernacle Street, London were burgled.

In 1975, following a police statement about the burglaries by A.N.C., three exiled African families, all associated with A.N.C., had their homes broken into over a period of 10 days. By contrast with previous burglaries, all found valuables had been removed.

In February 1976, the hotel room of the administrative secretary of S.W.A.P.O., Moses Garoeb, was burgled. His suitcase and attaché case were rifled, sensitive documents were stolen, and papers were scattered about the room.

On 7th May, 1976, coinciding with A.A.M's arms campaign and its exposure of breaches of the arms embargo to South Africa, there was a break-in at A.A.M's offices. The door was forced but nothing was taken.

Intimidation and surveillance take many forms, but the evidence in my dossier on the relationship between the English Special Branch and South Africa is disturbing. In November 1971 it was disclosed that a Detective Inspector in the Special Branch, a man called Donker, who was responsible for liaison with the South African Embassy, had been removed from his post for having irregular contacts with an Embassy official, a second secretary, A. H. Bouwer. The brief for such liaison is, officially, 'criminal matters and the protection of individuals and property', and the Special Branch were under orders that any meetings must be reported both before and after they occurred.

During the course of an internal investigation into an alleged leakage of information to B.O.S.S. (details of which, incidentally, do not appear ever to have been disclosed), it came out that Donker had three unreported meetings with Bouwer. Donker denied that there were three; he said that there were only two and that they were both entirely innocent. At this time it was also being alleged that South African Embassy officials had built up relationships with the Special Branch which went well beyond their brief. In this context, it is interesting to note that Donker's predecessor was also removed from his job for receiving consignments of drink and cigarettes from the Embassy. It is also interesting that, at the time of Donker's demotion, his colleagues felt that other policemen were in an even more compromising position concerning their relationships with the South Africans.

Donker denied that he had ever passed on information to the South Africans. While head of liaison, he established regular contact with an official of the A.A.M. He appeared in their offices and would ask for details of their future activities. The police were always informed of these anyway. Donker explained his contacts with A.A.M. by saying that he was trying to protect A.A.M. which, he said, he supported, from attempts to infiltrate it.

One of the accusations has been that there occurred a fairly extensive exchange of mutually useful information between the two authorities. For instance, an incident at Dover in May 1972 when a S.W.A.P.O. official, Ewald Katjavena, on one of his many visits to London for consultations, was detained for four hours by the immigration authorities. The particular immigration officer involved was very hostile and appeared to be very well informed as to his identity, the purpose of his visit, and his address when in England. Documents in his possession were photocopied, his diary was examined and notes made of its contents.

One of the more subtle fields in which the South Africans

operate in England was exposed by Adam Raphael in 1974 in a series of articles which he wrote for *The Guardian* on British organizations which were being financed or in some other way controlled by South African interests. One of those he exposed was the Club of 10, run by a man called Sparrow. Through Delport, the Embassy's Information Officer (and, it appears, a resident B.O.S.S. man), the South Africans denied this. Raphael then got hold of a message from Pretoria to the Embassy giving the text of an advertisement to be placed in the British press some four or five days later. Subsequently, Raphael's briefcase was rifled and a file stolen from it – the document however was not in the briefcase.

A series of public allegations have been made over the last ten years about B.O.S.S. activities in Great Britain. Questions have been asked in Parliament many times. However the only time at which there has been officially stated acceptance of B.O.S.S. operations over all this period was in 1972. On 24th August, Mark Carlisle, then Minister of State at the Home Office, wrote in a letter: 'All I can say is that the appropriate authorities know that the South African Intelligence Service has been active in collecting information about anti-South African organizations and individuals in the United Kingdom and that they are keeping a watchful eye on those activites here.'

I have compiled similar files on right-wing and racialist organizations in Britain which proved to be particularly valuable at a time when the National Front and even more openly Nazi groups were taking advantage of various issues but, above all on the fears engendered by immigration. There were groups such as Column 88, the existence of which was only acknowledged after a Court case in Birmingham involving a fight between two members and an infiltrator. Until then it was supposed it was just another invention to discredit the far right or the figment of a paranoid imagination. The British Movement based in Liverpool, which boasted the membership of Colin Jordan, was exposed as a particularly vicious group. It is no secret that the violence in my own Constituency was linked with men with Liverpool accents, and when a National Council for Civil Liberties meeting was broken up (a young man was slashed across the face and an old lady's arm was broken) there was a similar connection. That group has connections with Ulster extremists and although only small, is separate from less openly Nazi groups. The interesting thing about the admirers of Adolf Hitler in Column 88 is that one can join them only by invitation. This means a good deal of persistence and ingenuity is needed to penetrate their ranks. Another such organization is S.S. Wotan, linked with letter bombs. The British Movement has grown in the wake of National Front divisions at a time of high unemployment.

The Ku Klux Klan, on the other hand, drew more interest from the press, and my own file expanded to the point where I was able to write about them. The magazine *Searchlight*, which specializes in this work, was an invaluable source of information. What was astonishing was the way in which our immigration authorities and the Home Office, so quick to pounce in other cases, could allow American Nazis and Klansmen to come over and preach their gospel of hate in 1978. Dave Duke made a fool of the Home Office who did not appear to know anything about him. That was curious since I had only shortly before referred to him in published articles and in interviews for the press, radio and television. That the Home Office could be so blind over South Africa or Nazi fanatics contrasted curiously with their attitude to interfering radicals.

That none is so blind as the Home Office when it does not wish to see is illustrated by two topics with which I became associated in my early and my late years at Westminster when Labour was in power: Northern Ireland and the growing danger of pseudo-religious cults, a topic which is increasingly occupying the attention of the media as its full ramifications are revealed.

CHAPTER TWELVE

The Northern Ireland Fiasco

On no topic were my fears more well-founded and my frustrations at being ignored more justified than on Northern Ireland. How I became so involved and why I am now the author of two books on Irish history, one written with Patrick Quinliven (who unlike me is of Irish descent), all resulted originally from a talk on civil liberties to an Irish group in Manchester, in 1962. What I learned there made me resolve to visit the province and when I was asked about Northern Ireland at the 1964 Election I gave a solemn undertaking to do so. A year later I was to found the Campaign of Democracy in Ulster, largely inspired by the Dungannon-based Campaign for Social Justice led by Dr. and Mrs. McCluskey who attended our first meeting at the House of Commons. My principal Parliamentary ally at that time was Stan Orme, my neighbour from Salford who later became a Junior Minister for the province.

A number of M.P.s gradually came to our side, such as Liverpool members Eric Ogden and Eric Heffer, and old campaigners like Lord Brockway and Hugh Delargy. A groundswell of support grew as we achieved the distinction of having a hundred sponsors from both Houses. The Secretary, Paddy Byrne, was always a tower of strength and while many Catholic Members were pleased at our actions, the campaign was led most vocally by non-Catholics within the House. One irritant was the factor of the tiny Labour majority which would have been trebled but for the Ulster

Unionists who at that time were an integral part of the Conservative Party.

Our main problem was to penetrate the blank wall of incomprehension and ignorance about Ulster. Members who knew about Saigon or Salisbury seemed to know nothing of Stormont. Others were worried at the delicate problem of religious controversy in their own Constituencies, as the Chief Whip Ted Short told me. Even Roy Jenkins, with his sense of history, accepted that Ireland had been the political graveyard of many a politician. The fact was, there was a Parliamentary convention, erected into holy writ by Speaker after Speaker, that prevented us raising matters of real substance on the floor of the House without being ruled out of order. It prompted Hugh Delargy M.P. to ask whether we could discuss anything besides Harland and Wolff.

When I entered Parliament in 1964 the stirring of the civil rights movement was still below the surface of Northern Ireland politics. Nearly fifteen years and many deaths and maimings later, Westminister was involved in a shabby little deal to give more representation to Northern Ireland in exchange for Unionist votes to keep Jim Callaghan at Number 10. The Irish question has been tossed about by British politicians so cynically that one wonders at the restraint of leading Irish politicians over recent years.

The Northern Ireland issue was the first major cause I espoused following my election to Parliament; and it was on the latest Bill that I made my final speech before deciding to remove myself from the political scene. If ever there was a recurring theme, over nearly two hundred years of Parliamentary struggle, it has been the failure of successive governments to grasp the nettle of Ireland. To the average Englishman, Irishmen are good entertainers and sportsmen and literary figures, but they are often regarded patronizingly where politics are concerned. The sectarian bitterness in Northern Ireland is not seen as a legacy of past British policies but as evidence that Irishmen of whatever persuasion are congenitally unreasonable and should be left to knock hell out of one another.

The more sophisticated view, espoused by the bipartisan

policy of the Front Bench, is that an English presence is necessary for basically the same reason – to prevent such bloodletting. The paucity of initiatives, with the sole exception of the abortive attempt at power-sharing, reflects the fear of getting too involved. The truth, however, is that Ireland suffers from an English problem.

The first Home Secretary I encountered was Sir Frank Soskice. He was clearly out of his depth where Northern Ireland was concerned, but he and his successors could hide behind the conventions of the Government of Ireland Act. The new intake of Labour M.P.s, concerned at this denial of their ideals in their own backyard, tried again and again to raise the real issues. They reflected the new generation in Northern Ireland, now led by men like John Hume and Austin Currie, who are not prepared to knuckle under to the one-party rule of Unionism and the limited patronage of a discredited Nationalist Opposition. In that ferment the Campaign for Social Justice in Northern Ireland was the biggest single influence on responsive British M.P.s.

Expatriate Irishmen and the descendants of Irish immigrants have always played a significant role in the British Labour movement. Now they were joined and overtaken by M.P.'s and an increasingly aware rank-and-file, concerned at the grievances of the minority in Northern Ireland. It was in these circumstances that in 1965 I became Chairman of the Campaign for Democracy in Ulster and earned myself accolades and death threats, devotion and loathing to such extreme degrees that I could never have conceived of before embarking on the battle.

The highlight of the Campaign for Democracy was a visit to Northern Ireland by Maurice Miller M.P., Stan Orme M.P. and myself in order to speak to leaders of the various political groups. Although only the opposition groups would meet us it was a remarkable tour. In some areas we were met by bands and led to the rostrum set up in the middle of the town like conquering heroes. Even the pubs closed. In Strabane virtually the whole town turned out at eleven at night, and television cameras were thrust upon us at one in the morning. Having been with Barbara Castle at Bristol the previous day and snatched only a few hours sleep before leaving for Manchester Airport at 6 a.m., I then found myself invited to a party just over the border. It proved to be a long journey and an even longer return to our hotel. The owner was still at the Party. Driving was Austin Currie, later a Stormont M.P., and while I have frequently fallen asleep during other people's speeches, I fell asleep in mid-sentence while talking to him.

We were able to meet the Secretary of the Belfast Trades Council, Betty Sinclair, to discuss economic problems. We met a number of persons who came from various groups, from the Northern Ireland Labour Party to the Nationalists, who were commonly termed green Tories. The gathering we had at Derry, whose walls gave us a view of the future spawning ground of violence, was most significant. In effect, it was the embryo from which the Social Democratic and Labour Party was born. The irony of Derry was that by concentrating the Catholics in high rise flats in Bogside, the Unionist majority on the Council could be preserved. It also provided a bastion for violence when ultimately the explosion came.

That night the petrol bombs replaced submission to the provocation of the 'Apprentice Boys' march. I was in my own flat about to leave for a holiday the next day when John Hume rang me in tears to tell me of the eruption of violence. All our friend knew the danger of violence and wanted to see peaceful reforms. They accepted that peaceful reform was the object, not futile arguments about the border. That their pleas and our pressure at Westminster were ignored is another indictment of the inability of an insulated machine to act on time and act correctly or indeed to act at all.

That the Government was forewarned is shown by the contents of the report we made and presented to the Government following that visit.* (See Appendix) Our demand for some time had been a Royal Commission. The very setting up of a Commission would have shown that we were aware of the problem. Instead the Government allowed the traditional, highly provocative Apprentice Boys March to trigger off such opposition that there was the danger of the Ulster Police running riot in Bogside. In that context no one could blame the Government, for the initial decision to send in troops. And all because they ignored our report.

A further frustration at this time was the blanket denial by men now regarded as Unionist moderates that anything was at all wrong in the six counties. When Alice Bacon was delegated the task of overseeing Northern Ireland affairs, I remember how Kevin McNamara, M.P. and I were horrified at the way in which she swallowed the bait of Terence O'Neill. It was thought then that the best policy was to back these 'moderate' men of the ascendancy, later rejected by the very masses they had misled under the blanket of the Union flag. They represented nobody but the Anglo-Irish dynasty.

When I proposed an Ombudsman for Northern Ireland, the Labour Government was at pains to explain that this could not be done. When Harold Wilson eventually announced the creation of such a post, it was too late. The whole story of 1964–70 was that by acting too late, the majority backlash was allowed to organize and arm itself and draw out of the shadows the gunmen of the Provisional I.R.A.

The refusal of Westminster to ban the flagrantly provocative Apprentice Boys March led to the commitment of British troops to an area where traditional hostility would inevitably override the initial relief with which their presence was greeted. The emergence of the gunmen in the wake of sectarian attacks followed.

The first mistake behind the sympathetic and constructive rhetoric of Harold Wilson was not to grasp the nettle in his first year of office. He said enough to alarm the majority but did insufficient to satisfy the minority. The gerrymandering discrimination and one-party political domination went on unabated. Not even the civil rights marches or violence in Derry or the emergence of such a remarkable phenomenon as Bernadette Devlin disturbed the complacency of politicians lulled into inactivity by the habits of half a century.

Jim Callaghan cut an unflappable and reasonable figure among the crowds in Belfast and left office before blotting his copybook. Willie Whitelaw exuded reasonableness and affability, but the toll in death and destruction increased. Whatever the procrastination and faults of the 1964–70 era, the gravest mistake ever committed was the Conservative decision on internment. That was the equivalent of a recruiting sergeant for the I.R.A.

Merlyn Rees' failure of nerve over the first Ulster workers' strike was not mirrored by Roy Mason, but while Northern Ireland now has no Stormont and no Assembly, it does have a Minister. His role is to prevent the breakdown of administration and uphold the domination of the army. Not a single political initiative has emerged in the wake of Tory failures. Airey Neave, to be viciously assassinated, wooed Unionists while Enoch Powell put his faith in the permanence of the Union direct rule and supported Labour in power.

Meanwhile, beneath the surface, more and more Ulstermen are seeing themselves trapped in the triangle, neither relishing domination from Dublin or witlessness from Westminster. Tough talk from Roy Mason earned him the title of Napoleon. In fact, like his predecessors, his period of stewardship was unproductive. It institutionalzed inactivity. If Unionists of the Reverend Ian Paisley's ilk will not accept power-sharing in Northern Ireland, why should they be given increased power at Westminster?

Only acute insensitivity can excuse a Bill which emphasized the integration of Northern Ireland into the United Kingdom. At a time when devolution was being preached from Aberdare to Aberdeen, the opposite was being proposed for the only part of the United Kingdom which has a historical connection and geographical unity with another nation state.

If one positive and hopeful development has emerged from the successive miscalculations, mistakes and inaction by British Governments it is the beginning of new attitudes among a significant number of Ulstermen. They realize that, whatever their traditional loyalties, they are part of the same community. They have a common interest and exist within a wider economic community to which both Britian and Ireland belong.

If there is to be a new initiative it must have an Irish dimension without causing Unionists a sense of betrayal. It must involve all sections of the community in its institutions while recognizing that historical allegiances and cultural differences can exist without accusations of treason and subversion. Within the wider European context and increasing regionalism the old dividing lines may begin to blur at the edges.

To emphasize the Westminster link while taking no initiative to create viable institutions within Ulster that are acceptable to the minority is a recipe for continued bloodshed. Since 1964 successive Ministers seem to have learned nothing and achieved nothing. To make it worse, principle has now been sacrificed on the altar of expediency. No long term strategy exists. The troops remain and the killings continue. The problem is more intractable than in 1964 when decisive action to destroy the tyranny of an entrenched majority might have forestalled the backlash. The bankruptcy of all sides of the House is reflected in a Bill to add a few paltry seats in Westminster to Northern Ireland. The futility of years of action by a few concerned M.P.s is reflected in the small numbers willing to challenge this latest in a line of errors. If they cannot understand the symbolism of the move they will never understand the reality in an area where symbols can be more vital than reality itself.

I may have failed in Parliament to move Ministers but I shall always treasure one letter I received from Mrs. Patricia McCluskey of the Campaign for Social Justice in Northern Ireland.

The Northern Ireland Fiasco

Paul Rose, Esq., M.P.,
House of Commons,
Westminster,
London, S.W.1.

30 March 1973

Dear Mr. Rose,

On behalf of every member of our Committee I want to offer you our warmest thanks for all you have done for us, in the Campaign for Democracy in Ulster.

Your name will always be cherished by Irish people.

Sincerely Yours,

Mrs. P. McCluskey
For the Campaign for Social Justice in Northern Ireland.

CHAPTER THIRTEEN

Enough is Enough

In the light of all my political differences over major issues, it is ironical that my final battle with Government blindness to the realities of life was not directly political at all. It was over an issue which is becoming a major source of controversy in the U.S.A. and increasingly in Europe.

It was once again one of those complete accidents that led me into this particular minefield. In 1974, my then secretary had a friend whose son had joined a cult at Oxford and was giving up his studies and his personal property in order to devote himself to this new religion. Until then his life had been sheltered and he was extremely talented but unworldly. He had clearly been flattered by the attention paid to him by existing members.

I was next introduced to parents who had rescued their daughter in a hysterical condition from the cult's headquarters. Together with colleagues I ensured the rescue of another girl after a five-hour chat and meal during which I showed her all my documentary evidence and introduced her to someone who had seen the cult's activities at first-hand in the U.S.A. I obtained one document in the premises of the cult from a heap of discarded papers. Others were brought to me by ex-members or relatives of members. News and information poured in from all over the world as I became the target of those concerned with the issue. Thus, a minor matter grew and, like Northern Ireland, it became associated with me in the House. From the myriad of correspondents an organization was formed with an initial meeting at the House. It bore the name of Family Action Information and Rescue – F.A.I.R. It now has over a thousand Members and while non-denominational it includes Hindus, Jews, and freethinkers. It works

closely with evangelical Christians in the Deo Gloria Trust
and has close contacts with the Church of England Enquiry
Centre and the Evangelical Alliance. F.A.I.R. also has wide
contacts in the media, which have been invaluable in collecting and disseminating information. They have now helped
many disoriented youngsters break away from the clutches of
the cults or to dissuade them from joining.

It is, sadly, a significant commentary on the poverty of
ideology and spiritual vacuum among young people that the
growth of pseudo-religious cults has become a major phenomenon in the west. In the U.S.A. they have infiltrated 90%
of the University campuses and use remarkably sophisticated
recruiting techniques. It is sometimes said that religion has
become a major export of Southern California – a particularly
happy hunting-ground for many of the cults. Indeed, that
export has now become a major import into Europe and not
least into Britain. Its impact has been primarily on teenage
middle-class youngsters who are alienated from the values of
their parents and society but not attracted by existing evangelical movements or radical ideologies.

Indeed, whereas the 'guru' cult hit the U.S.A. in the early
1970s it was in the late 1970s that their tentacles spread to
Europe along with some home-grown sects. The difficulty
that faces alarmed parents, politicians and even some Governments is to decide where witch-hunting begins and legitimate protection from dishonest and dangerous practices
ends. It is hard to distinguish the extreme but honest and
dedicated fringe sect from the 'rip off' or the politically motivated and sometimes violent cults which may appear superficially similar. Nevertheless this is now a topic of major
concern in Europe. The former Home Secretary, Merlyn Rees
inexplicably, chose to disregard the evidence, or at least take
no action upon it while the Thatcherite commitment to individual liberty overlooks the deprivation of liberty implicit
in the 'brain washing' techniques of many cults – to say
nothing of their fraudulent methods of collecting money –
often under multifarious guises.

In some, sexual abuse, visa violations and suicides are a
cause for concern, and the mass murders and suicides of

People's Temple members in Guyana were an indication of the ultimate horror to which unquestioning devotion to a cult can lead. Nevertheless, cults go unmolested in Europe because of our commitment to freedom of conscience and religion, and more so because of the difficulty in proving illegal or criminal activity. There may also be a proliferation of linked groups under different names, running into hundreds, while the current advantage given to charities can allow a so-called religious organization to cover the business and political activities of these other groups.

One self styled second Messiah, has asserted

The whole world is in my hands and I will conquer and subjugate the world . . .
The present United Nations will be destroyed by our power . . .
The time will come . . . that my words will serve as law.

Some cults obtain their money through selling under false names or begging. The West German Government was so concerned at 150,000 youngsters having joined about a dozen sects that it proclaimed that their common aim in West Germany was the pursuit of power and money. All the cults named by them operate in this country and are notorious for their addiction to issuing libel writs. This is one reason why the media have feared to expose their activities as fully as is possible in the House of Commons where, however, there is a curious lack of interest. John Hunt M.P. attacked the 'Children of God' now known as the 'Family of Love' or 'Hookers for Jesus' – the reverse of the more puritanical sects. My own speeches and questions received bland and astonishingly uninformed responses from the Home Office. One began to suspect them of protecting the cults.

Shirley Summerskill commented, however, that 'We may as individuals take the view that the doctrines advanced are lunatic. We may be particularly suspicious of the motives of people who, while claiming to benefit humanity, have substantially enriched themselves. But these are matters of opinion' – again the emphasis on freedom of opinion. There are already many controversial cults in Britain. More are arriving every week and we are ill-prepared to combat their influence or to judge which are actually carrying on illegal activities.

Banding together in self-defence, several fringe groups have formed a society ostensibly to work for inter-faith tolerance and dialogue. More sinister was a fake organization called 'Power' which published a deprogramming manual and named anti-cult organizations including F.A.I.R. and individuals such as myself as supporters of its horrific techniques. At least one Home Office official and a Belgian newspaper were taken in by this 'black propaganda'. I traced the source and the culprit, clearly financed by one of the major cults, who did a moonlight flit from his London flat. Other forgeries such as a C.I.A. dossier 'on leaders of the anti-cult body F.A.I.R.' and false and forged invitations to a Deo Gloria Trust (a genuinely Christian Christian Evangelical body) conference testify to the sophisticated world of the cults which makes John Le Carré and Len Deighton plots look comparatively tame.

Organizations analogous to F.A.I.R. and Deo Gloria have been formed in France, the U.S.A. and in Australia and New Zealand. The pattern has become universal. A young Australian member of the small Ananda Marg sect committed suicide in Geneva by self-immolation while a German couple did the same in West Berlin by way of protest. In Britain, the suicides of members of various cults perhaps reflected the instability of many members of the cults rather than the influence of the cults themselves.

However, what concerns many parents and psychologists are the allegations of brainwashing made against some cults. The process was described by Marvin Calper, a Doctor of Philosophy and Clinical Psychologist in the U.S.A.

> Suppression of the individual's rational judgement process is fostered by sleep deprivation and sensory bombardment. Mobilization of guilt and anxiety in the indoctrinee intensifies this inhibition of judgemental processes and at the same time heightens suggestibility so that a child-like ego state is fostered in the individual. He is constantly manipulated and modelled by skilfully applied methods of indirect suggestion.

Professor John Clark, an American psychiatrist, stated that his research showed that:

> In the U.S.A. one third of the Moonie (Unification Church) recruits were schizophrenic. One quarter had personality problems and forty two percent were passing through the normal process of maturation . . .
>
> Unacceptable pressures were applied to potential recruits. Once brainwashed they were taught to raise funds. The motivation for the U.S. organizers is private gain and a lot of money is involved.

One must not of course extrapolate from the U.S. to the U.K. However, more violent results shocked the world with the news that the Reverend Jim Jones had armed his Guyana commune sometime prior to the slaying of the California Congressman Leo Ryan and the suicides and mass murders of more than 900 People's Temple members.

There has been no evidence of military training among Moonies but the *Detroit News* reports from the U.S.A. loyalty oaths to South Korea pledging military service against Communism and a readiness to kill for 'heavenly father' Moon if necessary. Whereas Moon is strongly anti-Communist, the Children of God have close links with Colonel Ghaddaffi of Libya and are strongly anti-American. Most cults have no political or military motive but Synanon, the California-based cult, has an 'Imperial Marine Corps' armed with handguns and rifles to 'protect' its members. 'The Way', a relatively unknown cult in Britain, is alleged to receive weapons training, and one active member is organizing a nationwide army of political activists with the avowed goal of putting men of God in the U.S. Government. This extreme right-wing body is active on high school and college campuses and yet avoids much of the publicity given to the better-known, albeit less violent cults.

More benign are esoteric groups such as the Emin which gives a sense of purpose and belonging to many London youngsters who might otherwise be lonely or disorientated. If membership is expensive it would be fair to say that, while many parents are concerned, there is no evidence of anything harmful or sinister in its methods or teachings. At Sandbach the Community of Yahweh has attracted criticism, but a local reporter concluded that members were sincere and unselfish. By contrast, two deaths of members of one small sect have led to public expressions of concern.

Extreme religious sects may well be no more than an attempt to recreate a truly religious highly disciplined and communal environment akin to the early disciples, and it would be wrong to jump to conclusions without evidence of malpractice. What is needed is a full enquiry by a Select Committee.

The alienation of young people from society, parents and dominant institutions accounts for the attraction of both genuine and spurious sects. Many join when abroad or away from home, in the absence of a supportive family. It is no secret that 'Family' is a much used – or abused – word in the cults. The horrific cult of Manson was known as the Manson family. One purely English cult came to prominence when its Midlands 'family leader' thrashed the bare bottom of a thirteen-year-old girl for looking at a boy.

In the U.S.A., on the other hand, a four-hundred-page report of a House of Representatives Enquiry catalogued the activities of Sun Myung Moon's Unification Church. In Britain there is a curious lack of awareness of the extent of the cult phenomenon for the media fear to expose the kind of news which is headlined in the U.S.A. However, a growing awareness is being demonstrated not least by Independent Television News and the Women's magazines, while *The Times*, *The Daily Mail*, and *The Daily Telegraph* are the object of a libel action by the Unification Church. The Guyana tragedy has highlighted on a large scale what Manson failed to bring home on a smaller one.

The cultural and political disturbances of the past two decades mirrors the years after the California gold rush when at least fifty Utopian cults appeared. Hippies, civil rights marches and the New Left have diminished as cults have spread. In the U.S.A. today there may be as many as 2 million youngsters in 2,500 cults. There, at least, the major cults are under investigation.

Investigation may be necessary in Europe too if only to distinguish the honest if eccentric cults from those using dishonest or dangerous methods. The North Korean and Chinese means of indoctrination of prisoners, without using violence, mirror the methods of certain cults. Others violate street vending laws and misrepresent the origin of their product and the destination of their money. Whether the objection be thought control or fraud it is vital that the public be informed. If a sect has nothing to hide it should welcome an investigation to avoid being associated with these criticisms. Curiously most of the major cults want to avoid precisely such an opportunity to state their case. One wonders why?

If all this sounds strange in the context of such subjects as Parliamentary reform, Electoral reform or Northern Ireland, it illustrates the difficulty facing an M.P. who wants to challenge the big battalions. By accident, I explored an area hitherto the concern of only a few people looking for a new angle. Geoffrey Johnson Smith had tangled with the Scientologists and came off best in the High Court. The then Minister of Health had taken action to restrict the entry of members to Britain. This has now been reversed in the House. The fairest way of deciding is to have a full open enquiry where all sides can present their case. After John Hunt fought the Children of God in the House of Commons, their centre of gravity moved from Bromley, but there is evidence of their return. My own battle was over a wide field but my main concern was with Sun Myung Moon. The Fraser report in the U.S. completely discredited him, and his organization has since had a violent shake up.

In resisting calls for an enquiry into this phenomenon, the Home Office again showed itself to be oblivious to the realities of the present day. Their knowledge was abysmal; they deliberately blocked any attempt to warn people and some voice a deep suspicion that there are members, sympathizers, and those who have been suitably placated by cults in places of power. Trying to penetrate this wall of simulated incomprehension and implied ridicule reminds me of my early days when warning about trends in Northern Ireland. I only wish I could put in print all that I know. Were there a Select

Committee then very many people could blow the lid off the horrific practices of organizations whose very secrecy makes them difficult to expose.

The successive attempts to influence Government in fields where I knew I had more information available than they was an important factor in my final decision to leave politics. The failure of the Labour Party to break out of a stultifying right-left squabble of increasing irrelevance was another. Above all the secrecy of Government and its power and patronage inflicted serious wounds. The deportation of a close and trusted friend who was a characteristic American radical was the turning point and embittered my relationship with the Home Secretary whose record on Ireland I regarded as abysmal. When he failed to fire a single shot over the bows of a cult making life difficult for me in a costly libel action, I became increasingly alienated. After all, this was the Department which interested me most. When my health began to suffer after fifteen years of intense activity I decided that enough was enough. This book is basically an expansion of the reasons for that decision and a description of the process that led me to enthusiasm and hope and then to disillusionment. Perhaps we should all stop and take stock after fifteen years. It is a pity that M.P.s cannot take a sabbatical year.

For during this year a great debate is taking place within and without the Labour Party. The split between National Executive and Senior frontbench spokesmen became public after a Party political broadcast. A new organization has been formed which clearly anticipates the possibility of a new Party. Shirley Williams, David Owen and Bill Rogers threaten resignation over Europe and The Party seeks a new formula for leadership election through an electoral college system. Roy Jenkins poses the possibility of a new radical centre party, although unhappily it sounds more centre than radical and is influenced more by the German Free Democrats than the Italian Radical Party.

I have strayed in time and been discursive in my approach. I may have been idiosyncratic in my choice of topics. I could have written also of experiences in the Middle East and tried to analyze the situation there. I could equally have devoted a chapter to the changes sweeping the Caribbean Islands. It would have been too easy to take Hansards from the shelf and reiterate long dead speeches. I have sought to do something else. There are enough text books and critiques of the Constitution. No one need look far for Party political propaganda. All politicians enjoy writing their memoirs. Personally I find the period painful in many ways but there are important lessons to be learned.

Indeed I feel guilty at opting out and distancing myself from politics and this account may amount no more than to a confession that politicians should have thicker skins, less scruples and fewer principles. If so, it is an unfortunate commentary on our democracy. While I may enjoy the civilized atmosphere of the Court and the frenzied support for Manchester United on the terraces, politics is like a disease which is capable of being controlled but not cured. There are new circumstances which could once again bring me back into the battle, but at present, quoting that arch-politician Harold Wilson, I will keep my options open.

Appendix

During the 14th, 15th and 16th April, 1967 three Labour Members of Parliament, Dr. Maurice Miller, (Glasgow Kelvingrove), Mr. Stanley Orme, (Salford West) and Mr. Paul Rose, (M/c. Blackley), visited Northern Ireland at the personal invitation of Mr. Gerard Fitt, M.P. Their objectives were to investigate the position in Northern Ireland with regard to discrimination, electoral law and practice, and the general economic situation. A further objective was to inform a wide spectrum of citizens of Northern Ireland of the activities at Westminster of Labour Members interested in Northern Ireland affairs.

They visited Belfast, Coalisland, Dungannon, Strabane and Derry. In Belfast, they met the executive of the Northern

Ireland Labour Party, senior shop stewards from Short Bros. and Harland, and the officers of the Belfast Trades Council. They also held a well-attended Press Conference, and gave television and radio interviews.

In Coalisland, they addressed a large public meeting, together with Mr. Fitt, of over a thousand people. The meeting was chaired by the Nationalist Northern Ireland M.P., Mr. Austin Currie. In Dungannon, they met local Independent Councillors, and Dr. and Mrs. McCluskey of the Campaign for Social Justice in Northern Ireland. Another public meeting at Strabane was attended by nearly two thousand people. This was followed by personal talks with a widely representative section of the community.

On the Sunday they were met by leading representatives of opposition groups, including Liberal, Labour Rep. Labour, Nat. Democratic Party, and leading independent figures from the city of Derry.

The party visited Derry, where aspects of housing and gerrymandering were examined and discussed. They met and exchanged views with the Derry Labour Party. Later in the afternoon, they had a short meeting, chaired by John Hume, and attended by two hundred representatives of all the aforementioned parties, and one Unionist. The Unionist Party officially refused to attend.

Impressions and Conclusions

1. The visit evoked a warm response and intense interest in a large section of the people of Northern Ireland.

2. Allegations of discrimination in housing allocations were examined. There can be little doubt that this exists on a wide scale, particularly where a dispersal of the population would result in a changed political balance as, for example, in Derry.

3. Discrimination on political and religious grounds is alleged and substantiated by figures previously provided by the Northern Ireland Labour Party, and other sources, and confirmed by all those with whom this was discussed. This applies in relation to Government appointments, for example, in the legal profession, in local government, and in sections of industry. In the legal profession, for instance, there are only eleven Catholics holding judicial offices out of a total of 142. In many public bodies, Catholic, Labour and Trade Union representatives are excluded.

4. *In Derry* there is irrefutable evidence of gerrymandering in order to perpetuate minority control, and it is feared that proposed boundary changes may perpetuate this in another form. At present, the Corporation has eight Nationalist members with a 63 per cent majority of the population, whereas the Unionists have twelve representatives with a 37 per cent minority, and therefore control the city.

5. *The electoral* franchise which excludes 250,000 voters from local government elections, and allows business and company votes (up to six) is an anomaly in the U.K.

6. *Electoral* malpractices were alleged by many, including contestants at previous elections. One practice alleged was that postal votes were forged so as to prevent anti-Unionists voting at election time. Another was that polling booths were deliberately situated in Unionist areas to intimidate non-Unionist voters. (The inflamatory nature of some propaganda, e.g. *Protestant Telegraph*, demonstrates how near the surface violence lies in current political life.) Personation is alleged to be widespread.

7. *Unemployment* varies between under two and over thirty percent in various areas. Catholic areas, and more particularly the areas west of the Bann, e.g. Derry and Strabane, are affected most. Urgent help is needed for areas like Strabane were 29½ per cent of the male population is unemployed. There are also pockets like Newry within the more prosperous areas.

8. *Short Bros. and Harland* presents a particular problem. The firm is a modern aircraft firm which is also greatly diversified, but its main product is aircraft. The firm has 65 per cent of public money invested in it. It has the most modern plant and machinery, and its technical and apprentice training is of the first calibre. This produces a technological fall-out vital

for British industry. A firm decision should not be taken to obtain suitable long-term aircraft work, and following the Plowden Report, this firm should be brought under full public ownership and developed as a modern science-based industry.

9. *Neglect* of the area west of the Bann is evident. The siting of the University and the New Town, and the run down of industry contribute to a situation where little development is taking place. It is widely considered that the Government of Northern Ireland's decision in favour of the New Town of Craigavon rejected the revitalization of Derry because of political motives. Derry, with its sea port and airport, could be made a new growth centre, acting as a magnet to draw industry and population to the west. On current trends, development will be one-sided, and restricted to the Colraine triangle.

10. *Small meat* farmers are experiencing difficulties since the Anglo-Irish Free Trade Agreement.

11. *Grants* and loans such as those foreshadowed in the Green Paper on Development Areas, and the Budget proposal to make available £50 million from the Public Works Loans Board (which includes housing development) are welcome, but must be applied in such a manner that there be no discrimination in the application of such sums for development.

12. *Unionist* reaction to the visit was hostile and provocative. The party was described as 'anti-Ulster', and 'interfering and unwelcome'. The Unionists refused to meet the members of the party, although invited to meet them on both the Saturday and Sunday. The pretext that they could not meet on a Sunday was a political manoeuvre intended to raise the sectarian issue and discredit the party in the eyes of devout Protestants. It ignored the fact that they could have met the party on the Saturday, and that all but the Unionists attended the meeting in Derry.

13. *There was* a ready response at all the meetings to the simple statement of principle that the Members of Parliament demanded the same rights and privileges for Northern Ireland as in their own constituencies as an integral part of the United Kingdom. A policy which respects the right of Irishmen un-

timately to decide their constitutional status for themselves, but recognizes Westminster's overriding obligation to ensure democratic government in the province is one which would commend itself to large sections of people, both Protestant and Catholic in Northern Ireland.

It is therefore considered that the Government should set up a Royal Commission to investigate the operation of the Government of Ireland, and the Ireland Acts.